FOR ORGANS, PIANOS & ELECTRONIC KEYBOARDS

E-Z PLAY TODAY

122

SONGS FOR PRAISE & WORSHIP

CONTENTS

2   All Hail King Jesus

4   As the Deer

6   Awesome God

8   Behold the Lamb

11 Bind Us Together

14 Celebrate Jesus

20 Come Let Us Worship and Bow Down

22 Create in Me a Clean Heart

17 Give Thanks

24 Glorify Thy Name

26 Great Is the Lord

32 He Has Made Me Glad

29 He Is Exalted

34 He Is Lord

36 How Majestic Is Your Name

42 I Love You Lord

44 I Will Sing of the Mercies

39 Jesus Is Lord of All

46 Jesus, Name Above All Names

48 Lamb of God

54 Lord, I Lift Your Name on High

56 More Precious Than Silver

58 O How He Loves You and Me

60 Oh Lord, You're Beautiful

64 Open Our Eyes

66 The Power of Your Love

70 Seek Ye First

51 Shine, Jesus, Shine

72 There Is a Redeemer

74 This Is the Day

84 We Bow Down

76 We Will Glorify

78 We Worship and Adore You

80 You Are My All in All

82 You Are My Hiding Place

87 REGISTRATION GUIDE

ISBN 978-0-634-02950-9

HAL•LEONARD® CORPORATION

7777 W. BLUEMOUND RD. P.O. BOX 13819 MILWAUKEE, WI 53213

E-Z Play r Today Music Notation © 1975 by HAL LEONARD CORPORATION
E-Z PLAY and EASY ELECTRONIC KEYBOARD MUSIC are registered trademarks of HAL LEONARD CORPORATION.

Visit Hal Leonard Online at
www.halleonard.com

All Hail King Jesus

Registration 2
Rhythm: March or 8 Beat

Words and Music by
Dave Moody

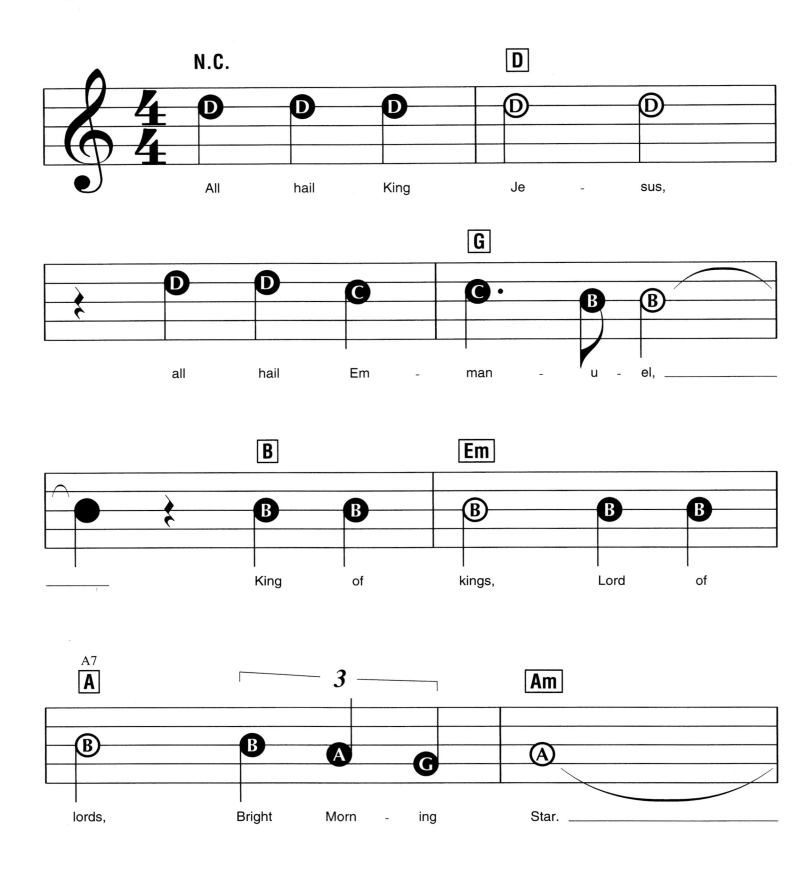

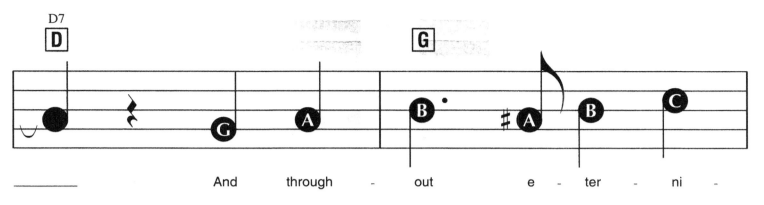

And through - out e - ter - ni -

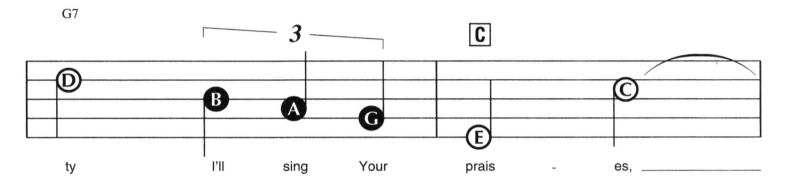

ty I'll sing Your prais - es, _____

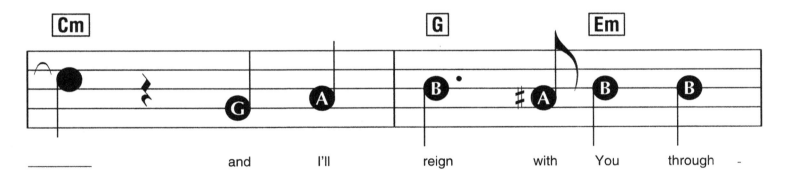

_____ and I'll reign with You through -

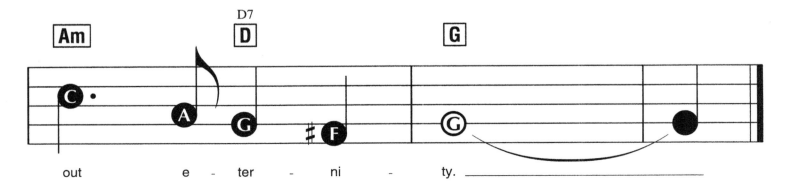

out e - ter - ni - ty. _____

As the Deer

Registration 1
Rhythm: Ballad or 8 Beat

Words and Music by
Martin Nystrom

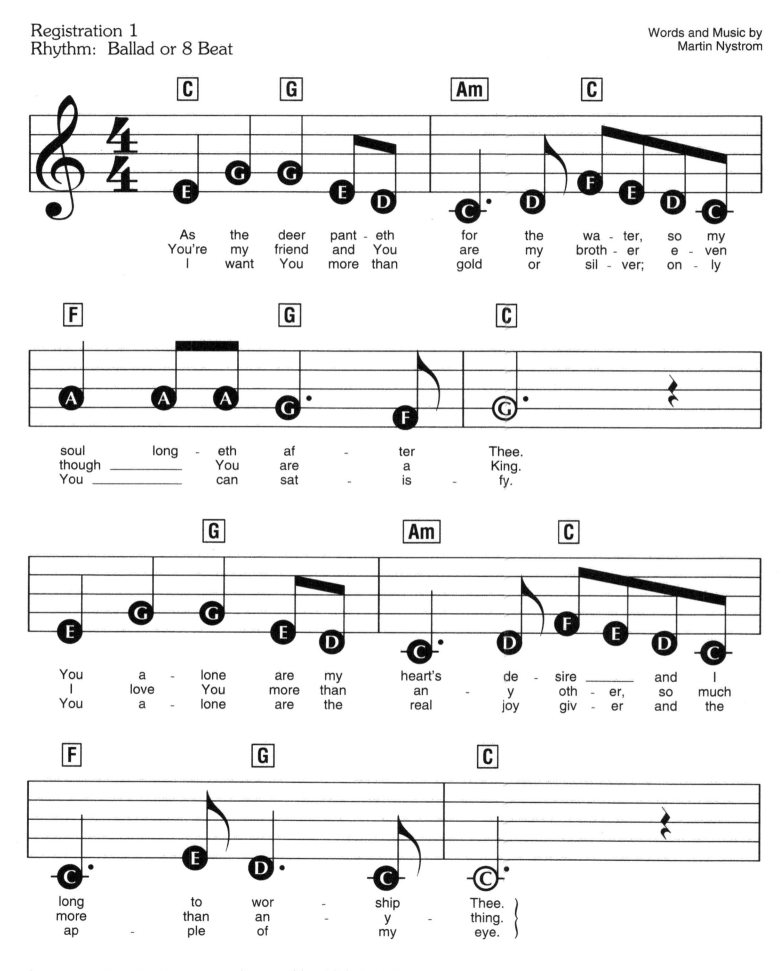

Awesome God

Registration 7
Rhythm: 16 Beat or Pop

Words and Music by
Rich Mullins

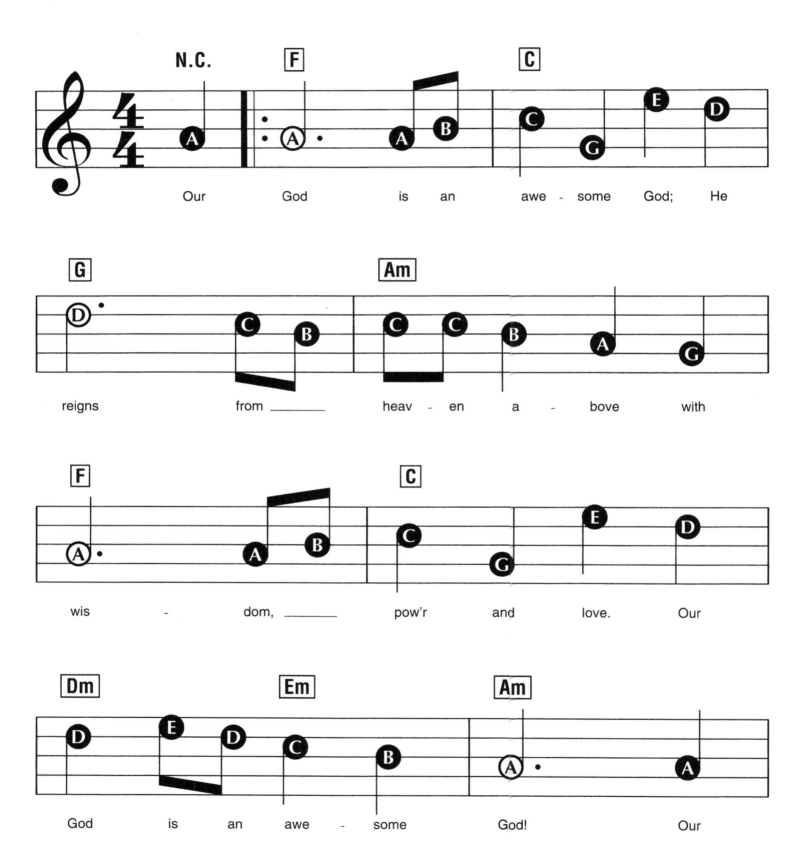

7

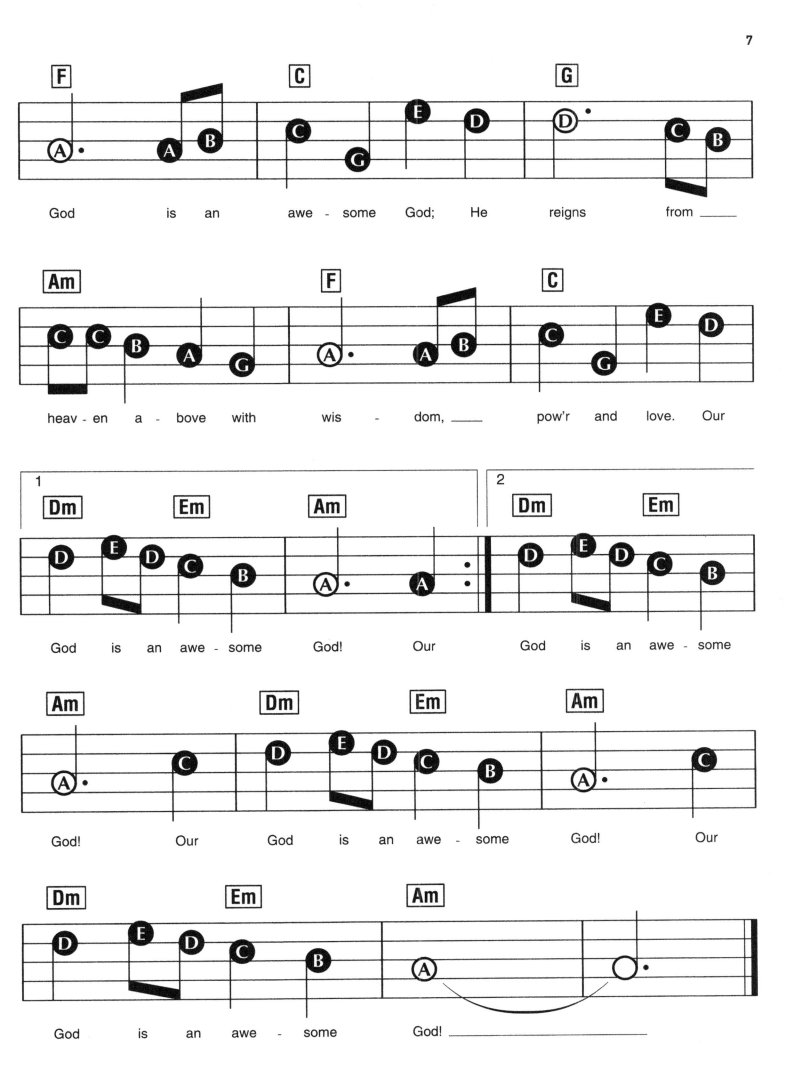

Behold the Lamb

Registration 3
Rhythm: 8 Beat or Ballad

Words and Music by
Dottie Rambo

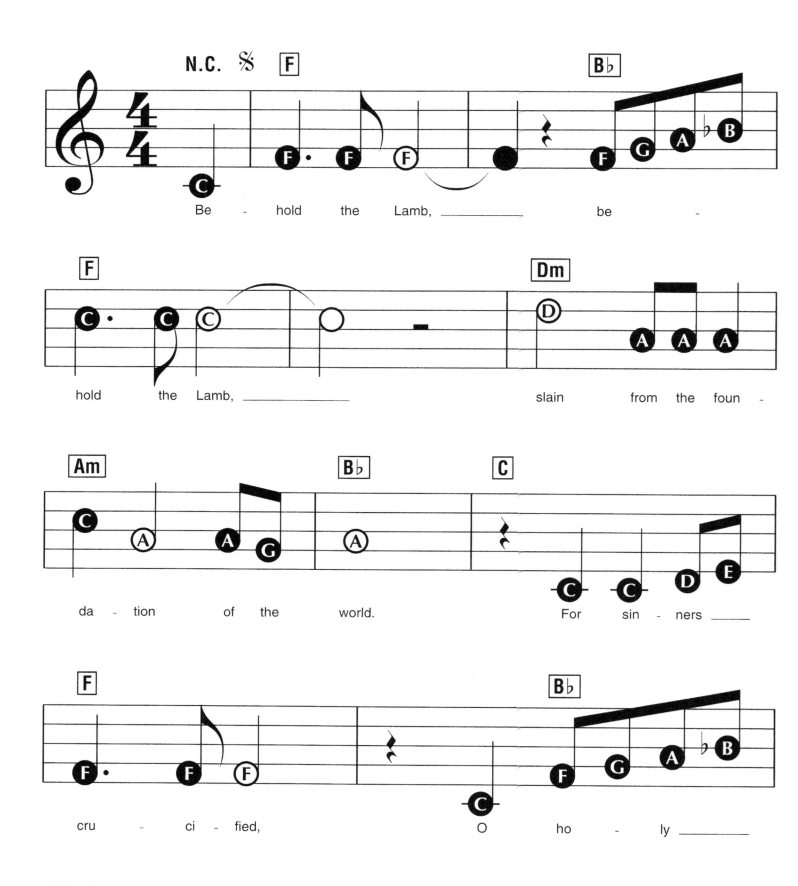

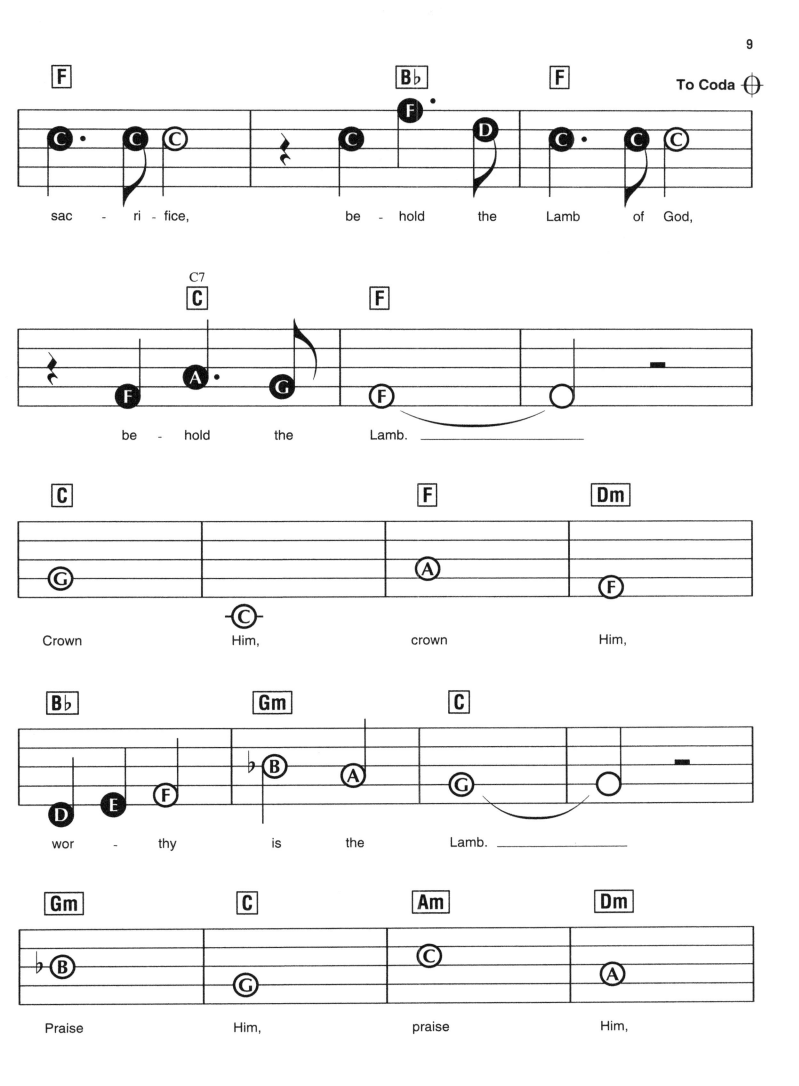

D.S. al Coda
(Return to ℅
Play to ⊕ and
Skip to Coda)

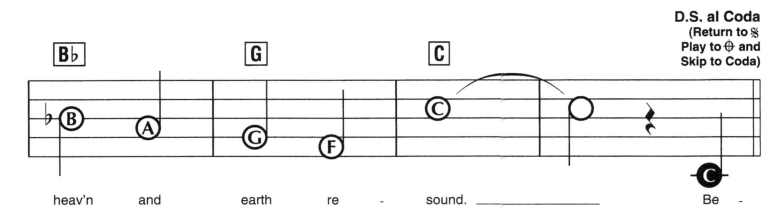

heav'n   and   earth   re   -   sound. _____   Be -

CODA

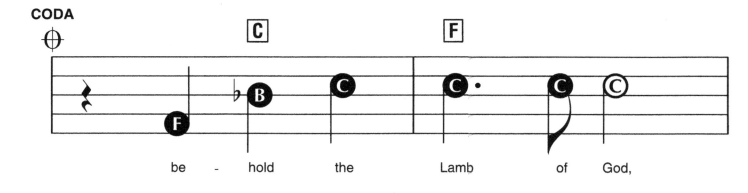

be - hold   the   Lamb   of   God,

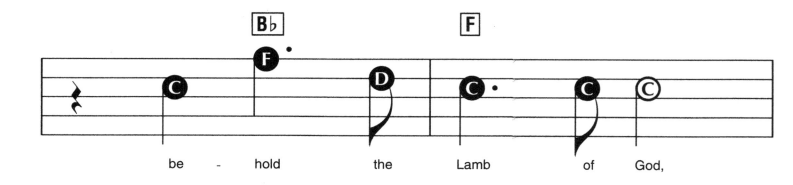

be - hold   the   Lamb   of   God,

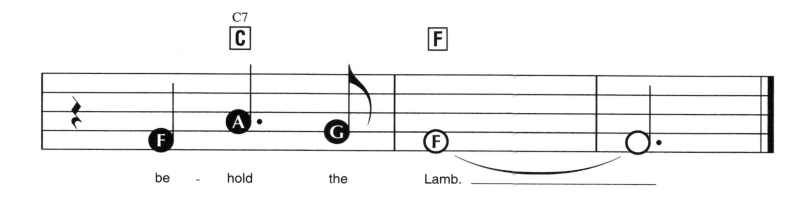

be - hold   the   Lamb. _____

Bind Us Together

Registration 1
Rhythm: Waltz

Words and Music by
Bob Gillman

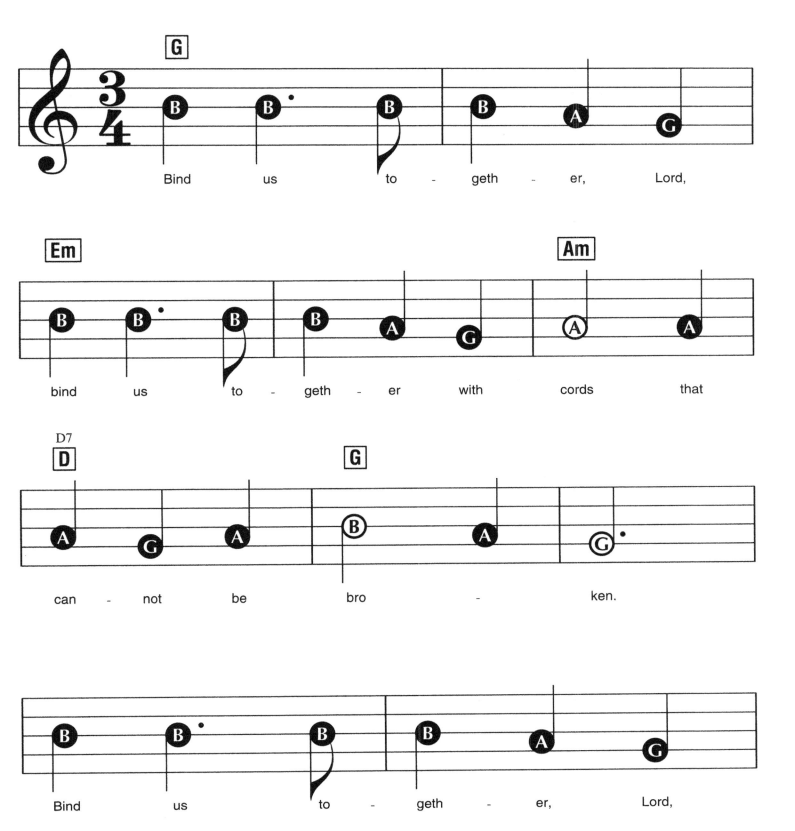

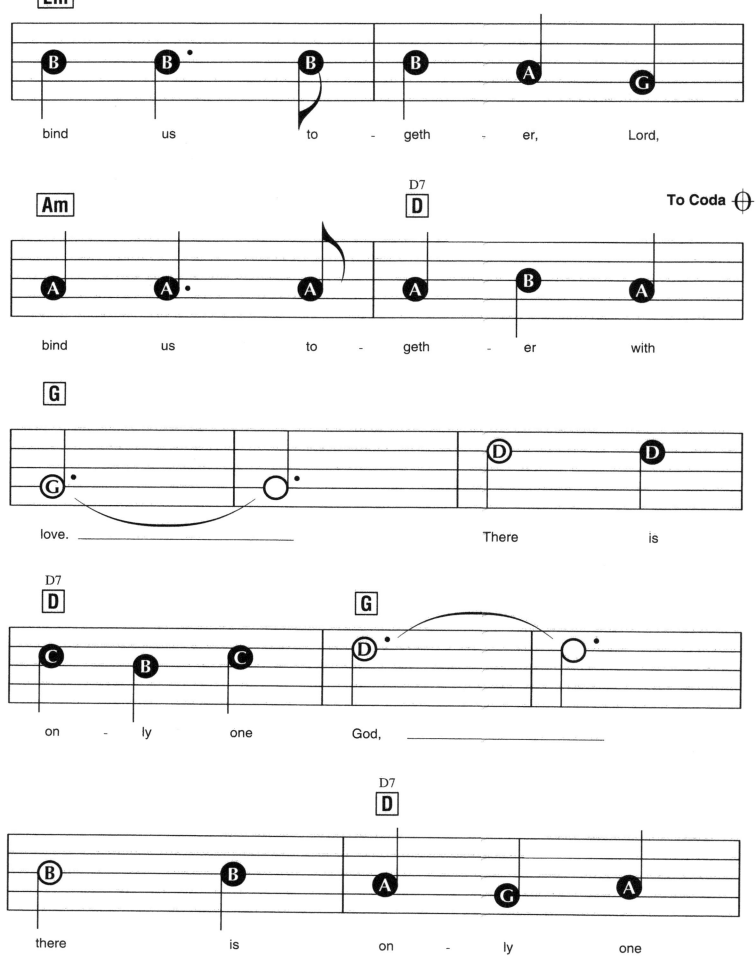

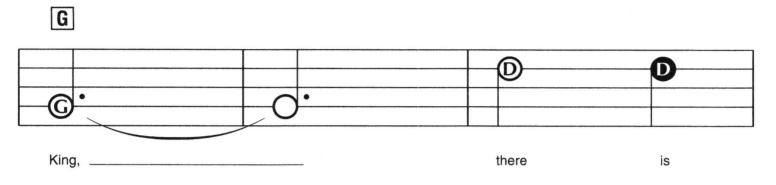

King, _____ there is

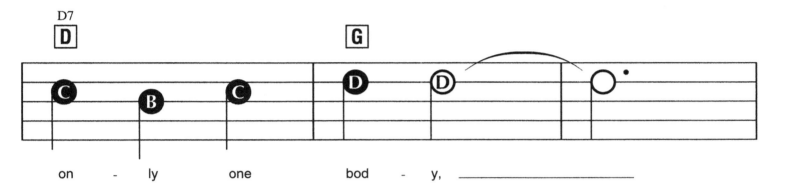

on - ly one bod - y, _____

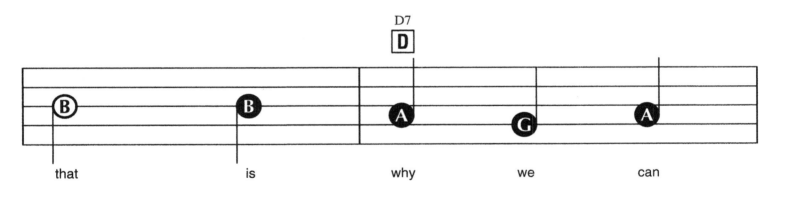

that is why we can

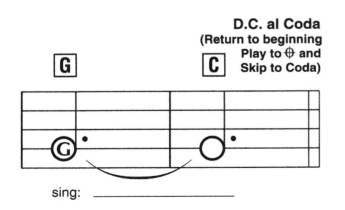

sing: _____

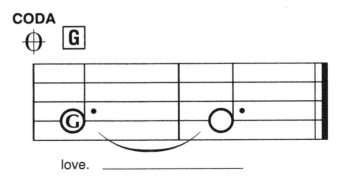

love. _____

Celebrate Jesus

Registration 7
Rhythm: Rock or 8 Beat

Words and Music by
Gary Oliver

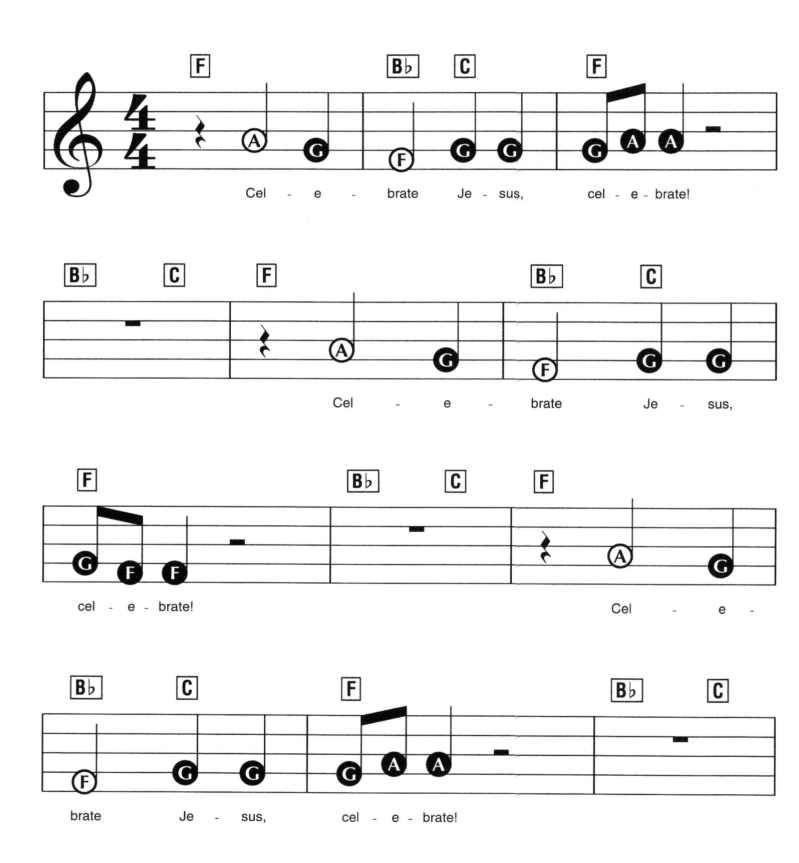

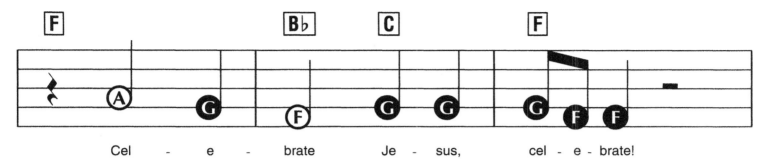

Cel - e - brate Je - sus, cel - e - brate!

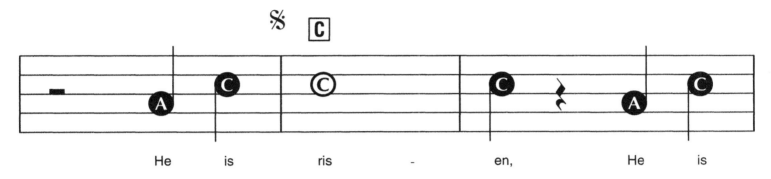

He is ris - en, He is

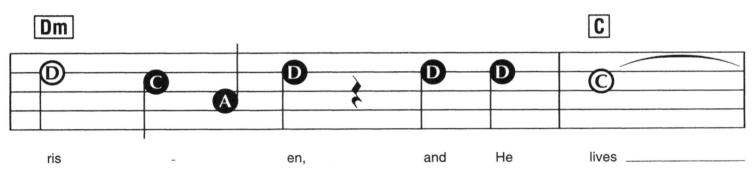

ris - en, and He lives

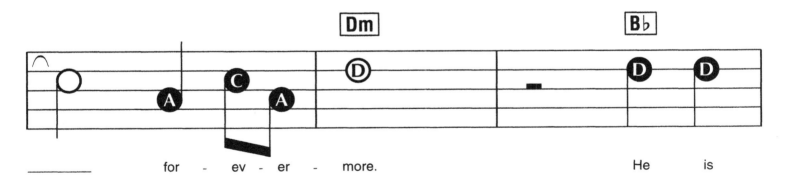

for - ev - er - more. He is

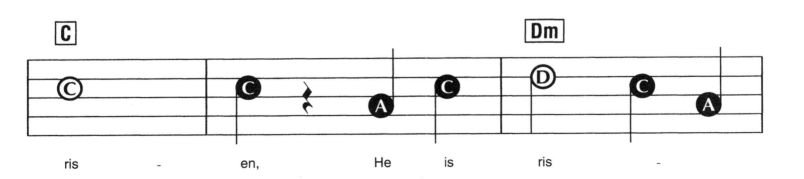

ris - en, He is ris -

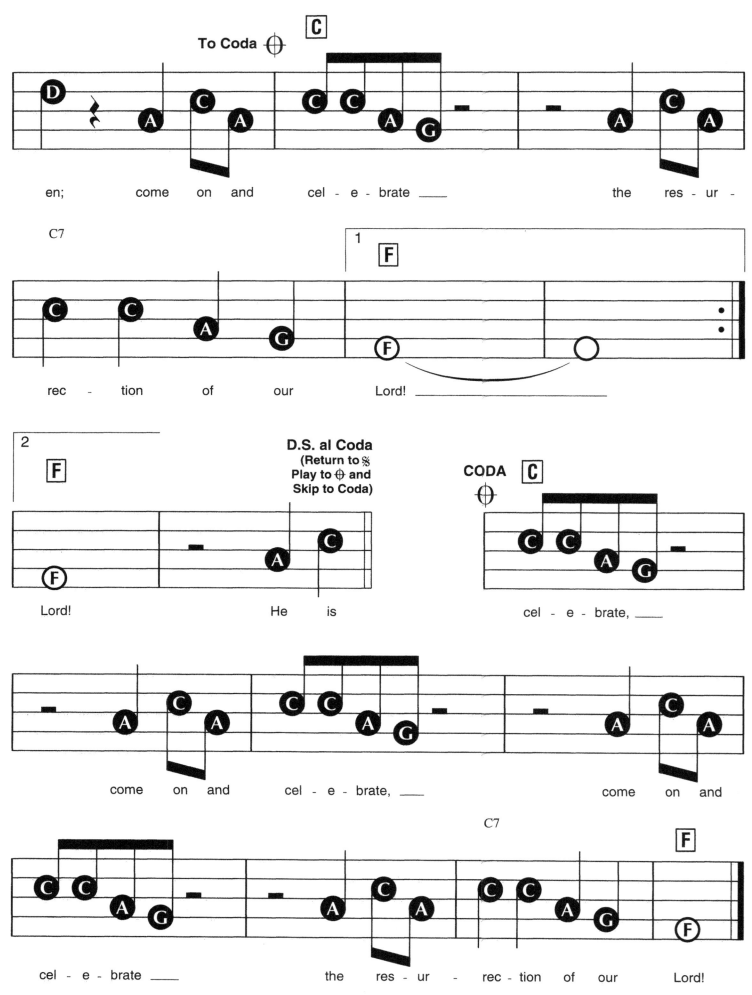

Give Thanks

Registration 8
Rhythm: Rock or 8 Beat

Words and Music by
Henry Smith

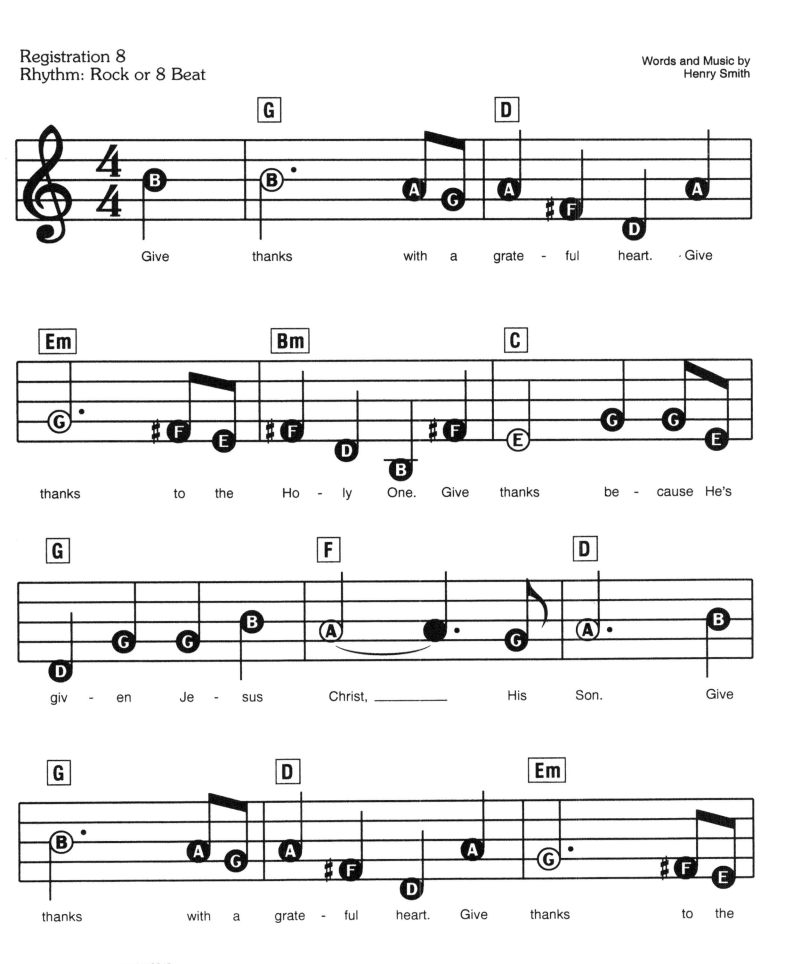

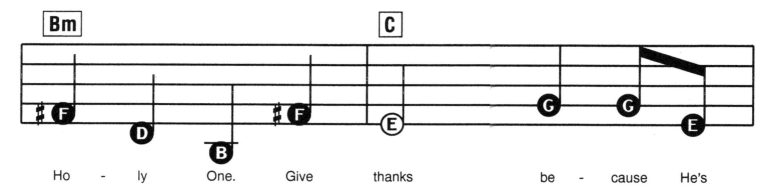

Ho - ly One. Give thanks be - cause He's

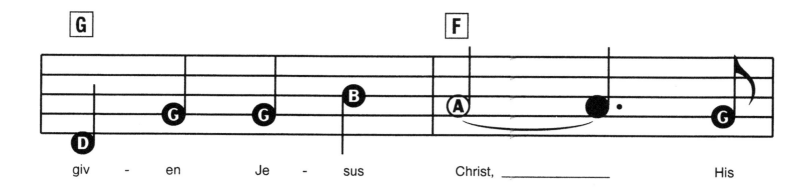

giv - en Je - sus Christ, _____ His

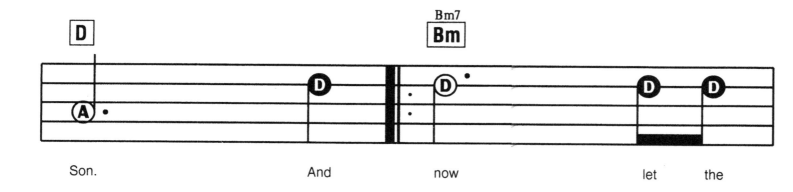

Son. And now let the

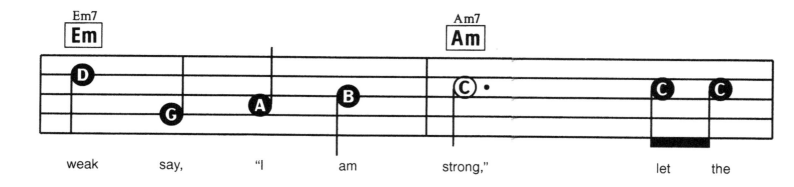

weak say, "I am strong," let the

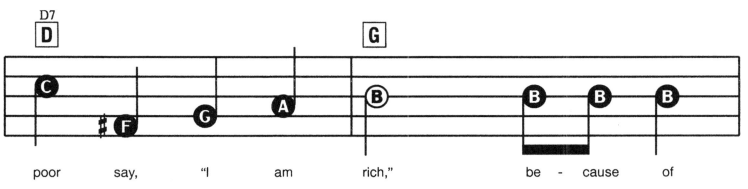

poor say, "I am rich," be - cause of

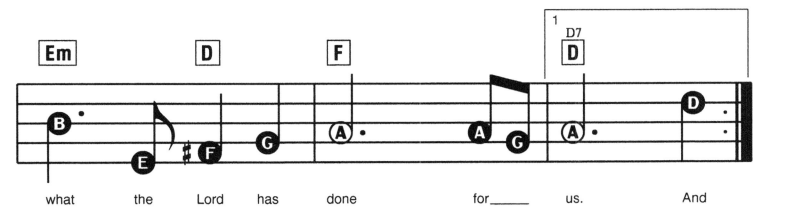

what the Lord has done for_____ us. And

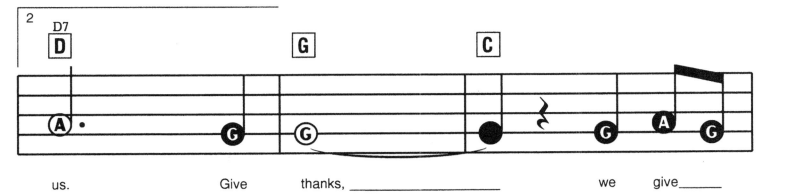

us. Give thanks, _____ we give_____

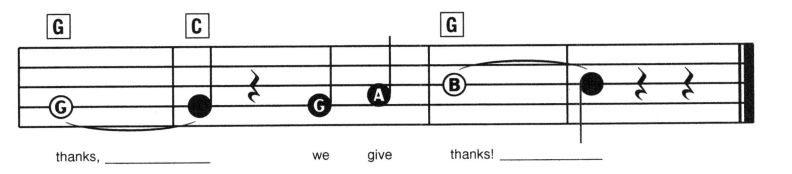

thanks, _____ we give thanks! _____

Come Let Us Worship and Bow Down

Registration 1
Rhythm: Ballad

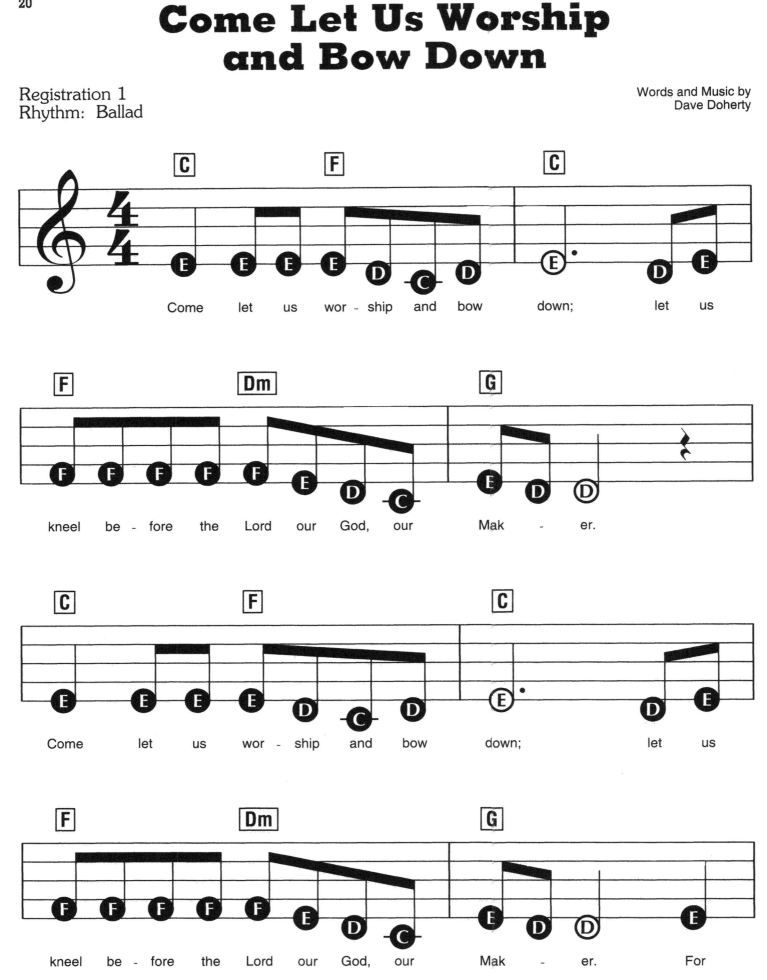

Words and Music by
Dave Doherty

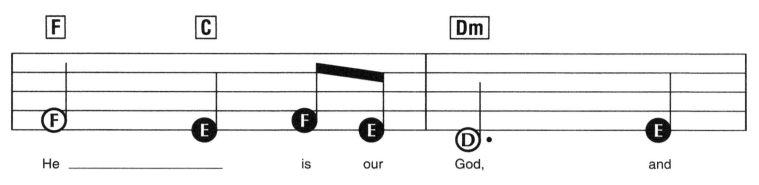

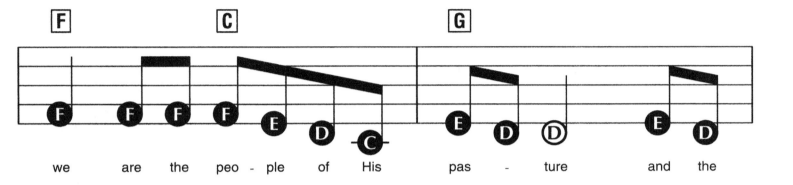

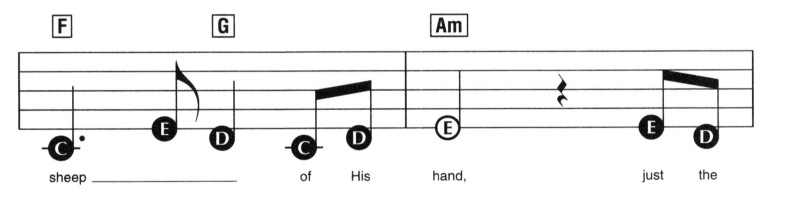

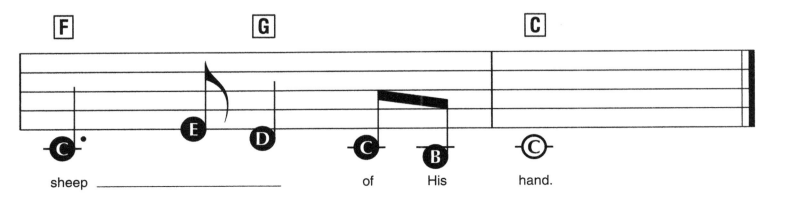

Create in Me a Clean Heart

Registration 8
Rhythm: Ballad

Words and Music by
Keith Green

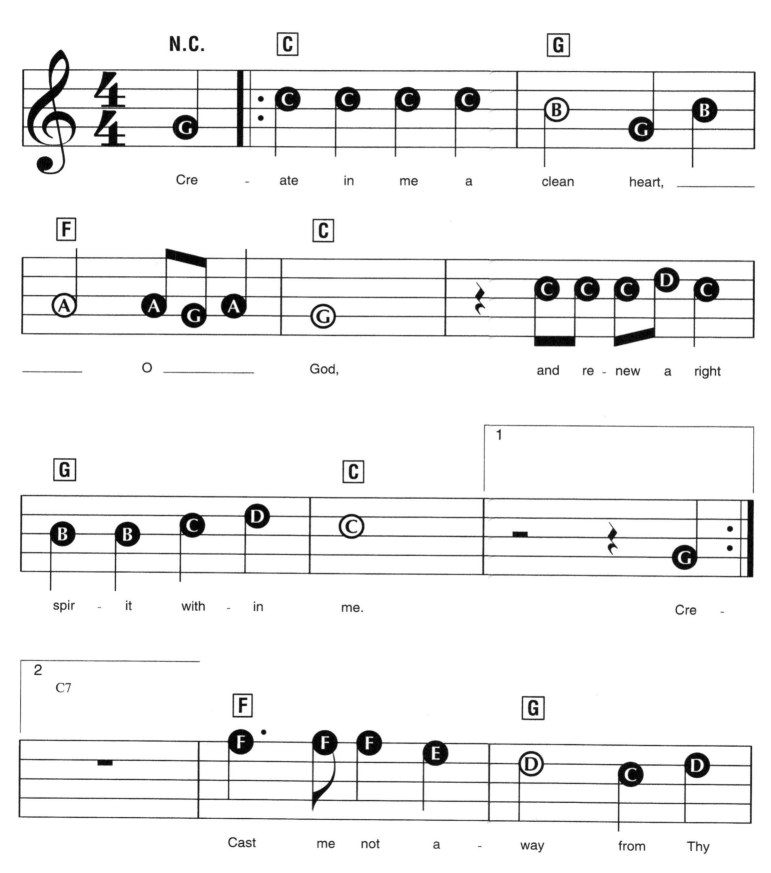

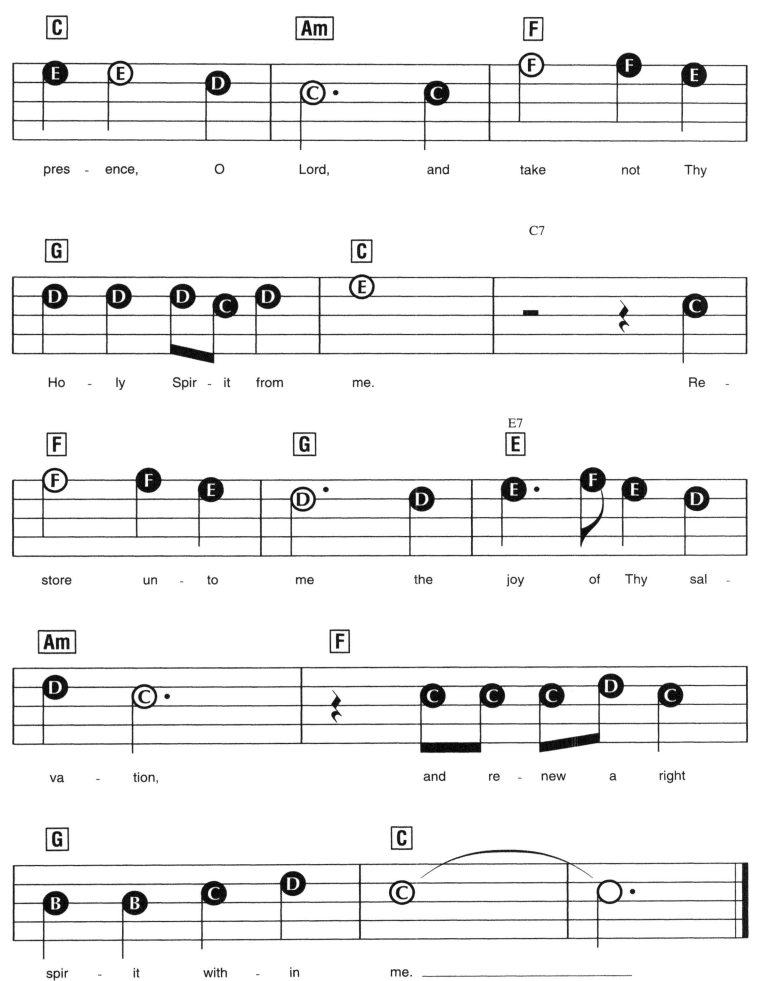

Glorify Thy Name

Registration 3
Rhythm: Ballad

Words and Music by
Donna Adkins

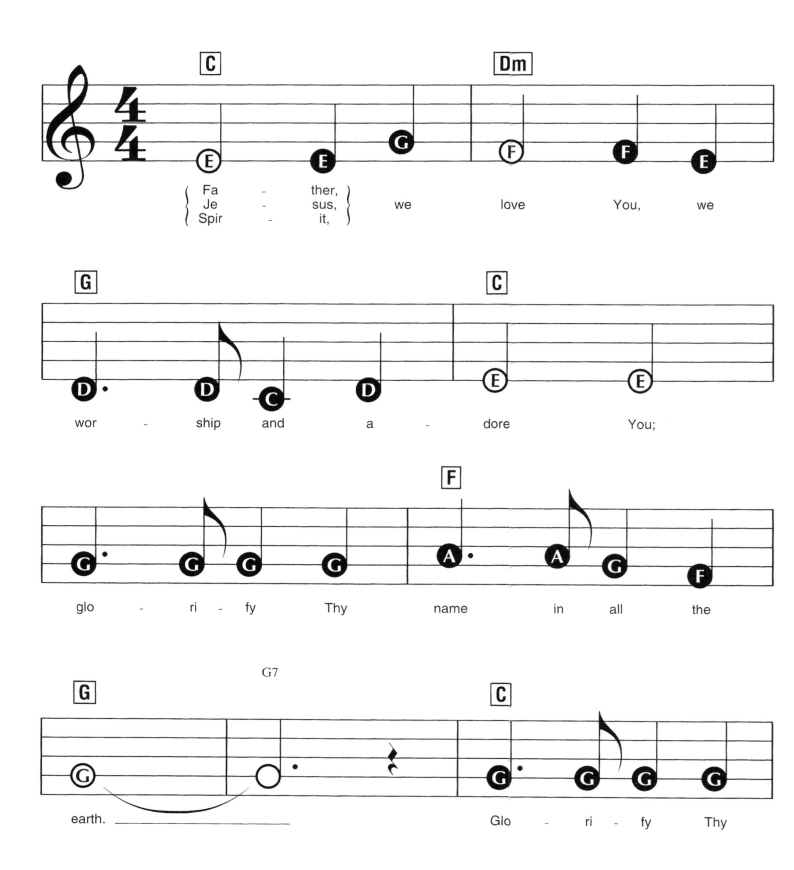

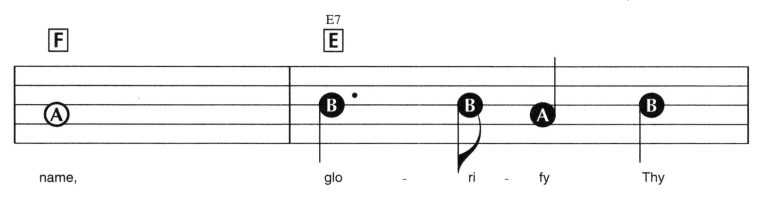

name,   glo - ri - fy Thy

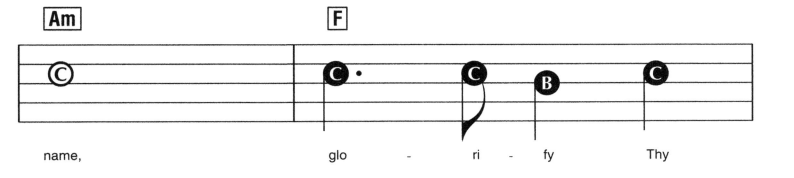

name,   glo - ri - fy Thy

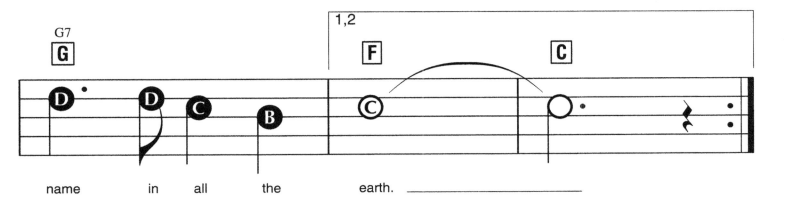

name   in   all   the   earth. _____

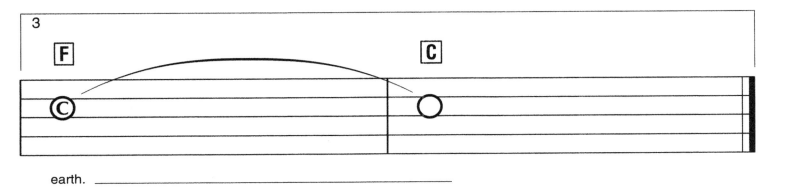

earth. _____

Great Is the Lord

Registration 5
Rhythm: Waltz

Words and Music by Michael W. Smith
and Deborah D. Smith

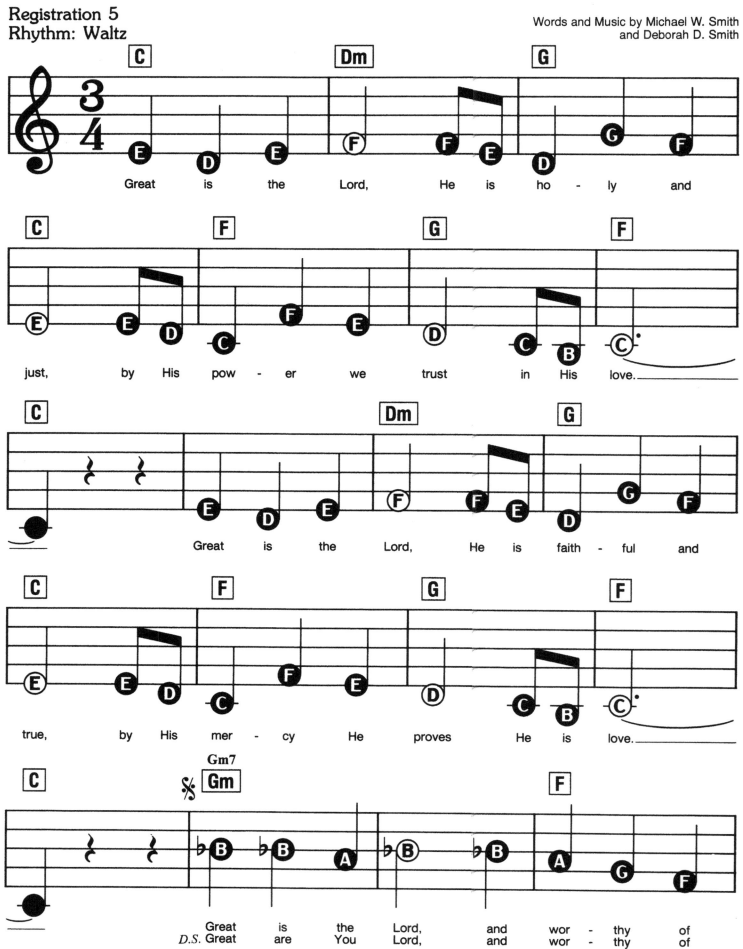

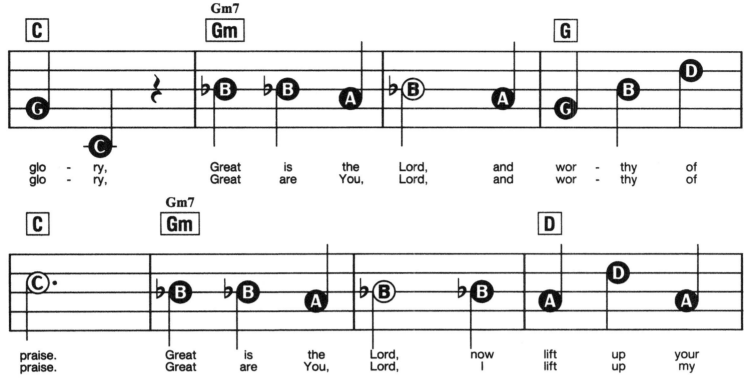

glo - ry,   Great   is   the   Lord,   and   wor - thy   of
glo - ry,   Great   are   You, Lord,   and   wor - thy   of

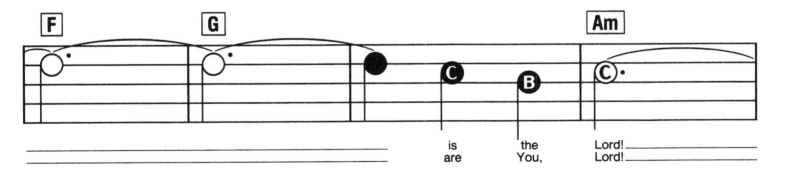

praise.   Great   is   the   Lord,   now   lift   up   your
praise.   Great   are   You, Lord,   I   lift   up   my

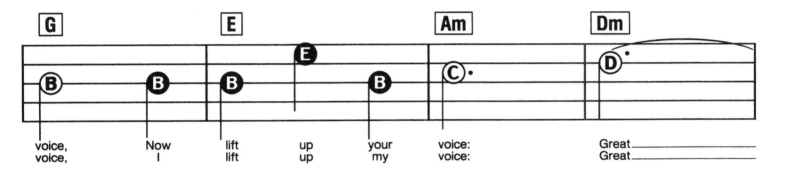

voice,   Now   lift   up   your   voice: Great_____
voice,   I   lift   up   my   voice: Great_____

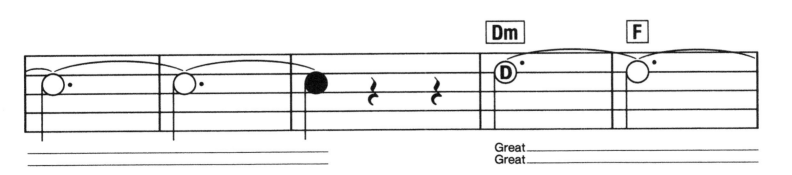

is   the   Lord!_____
are   You,   Lord!_____

Great_____
Great_____

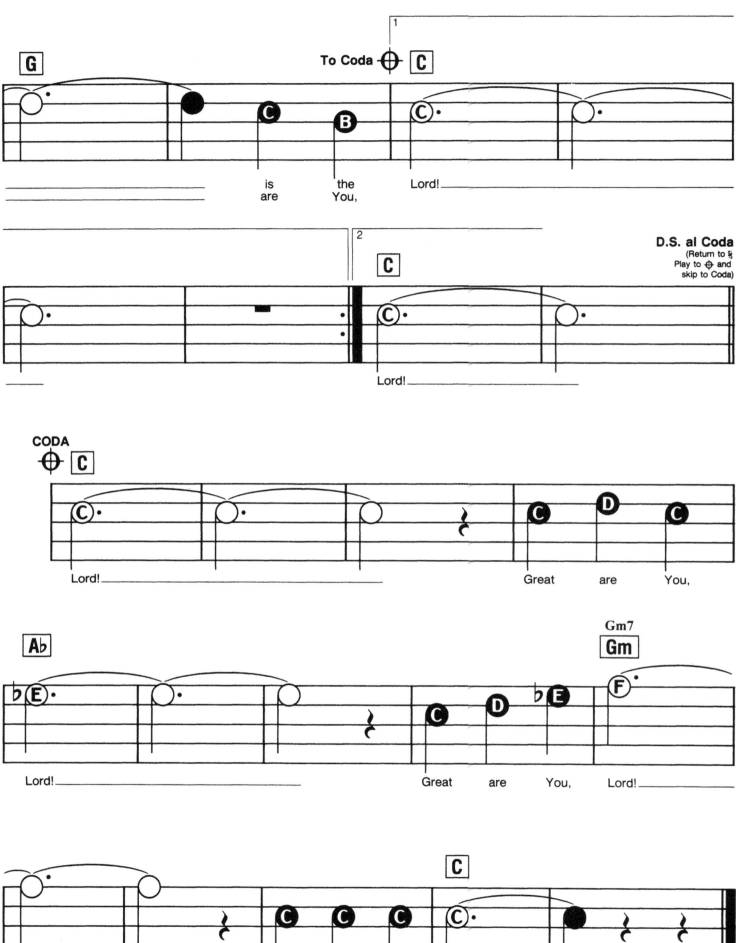

He Is Exalted

Registration 10
Rhythm: Waltz

Words and Music by
Twila Paris

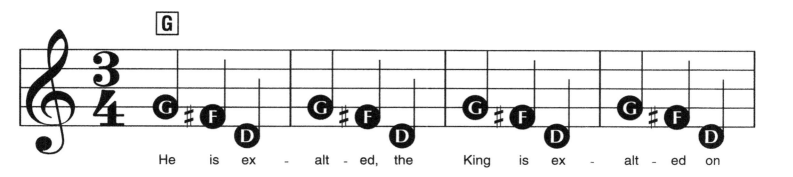

He is ex - alt - ed, the King is ex - alt - ed on

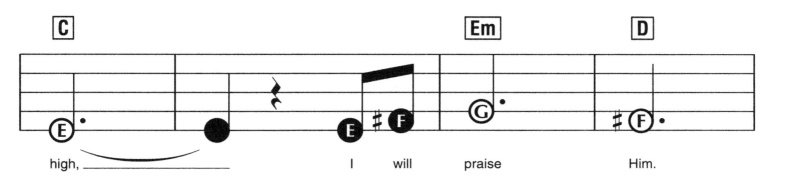

high, _____ I will praise Him.

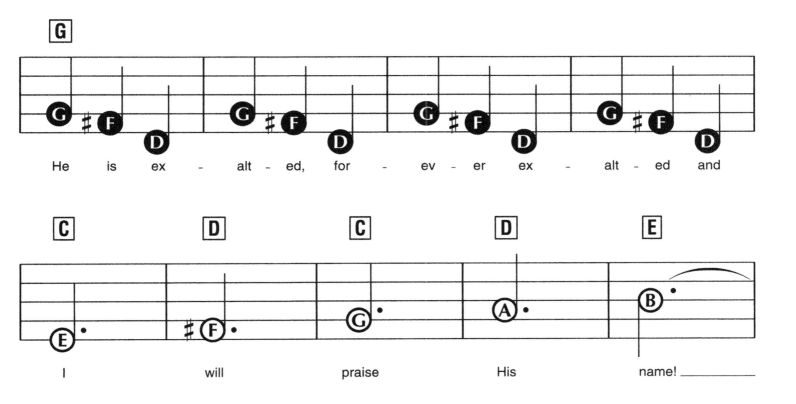

He is ex - alt - ed, for - ev - er ex - alt - ed and

I will praise His name! _____

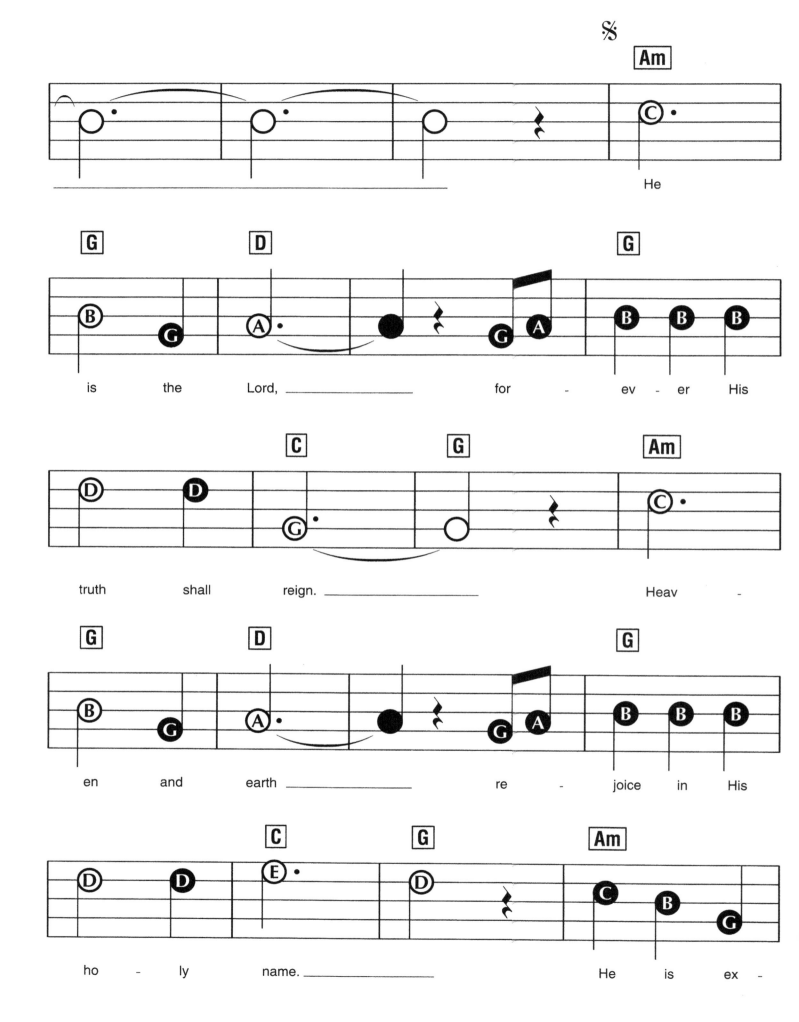

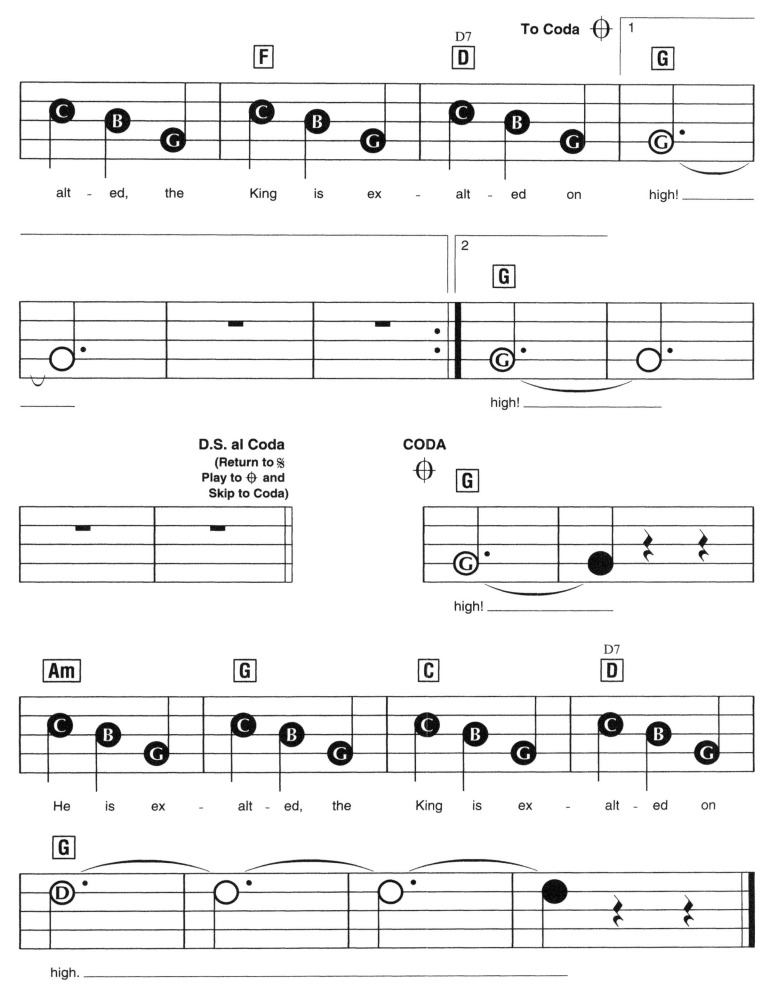

He Has Made Me Glad

Registration 7
Rhythm: Fox Trot

By Leona Von Brethorst

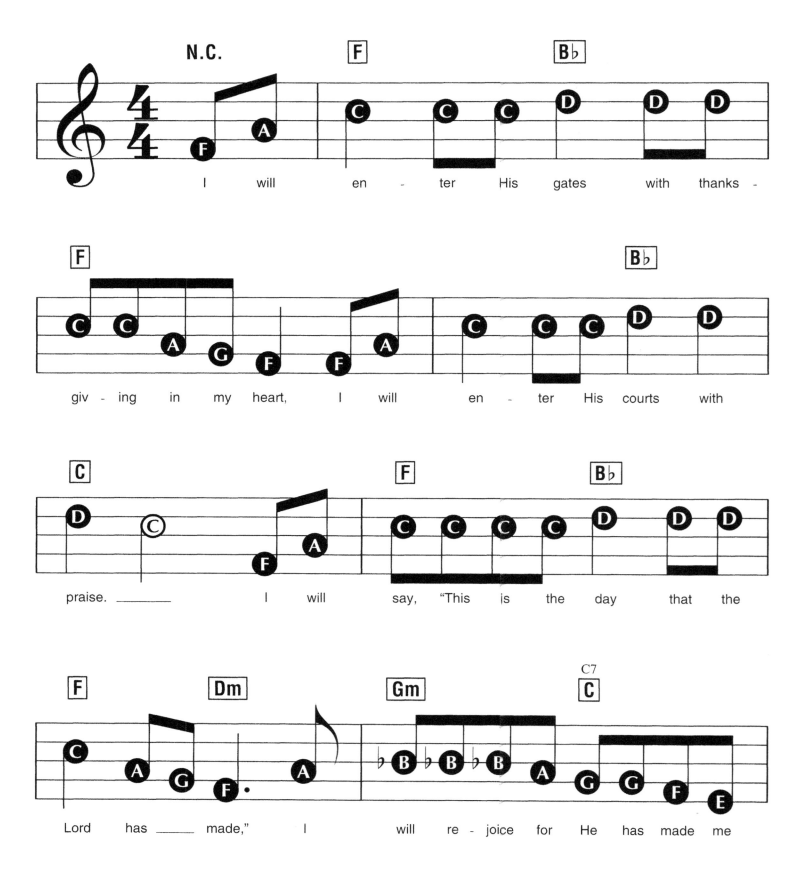

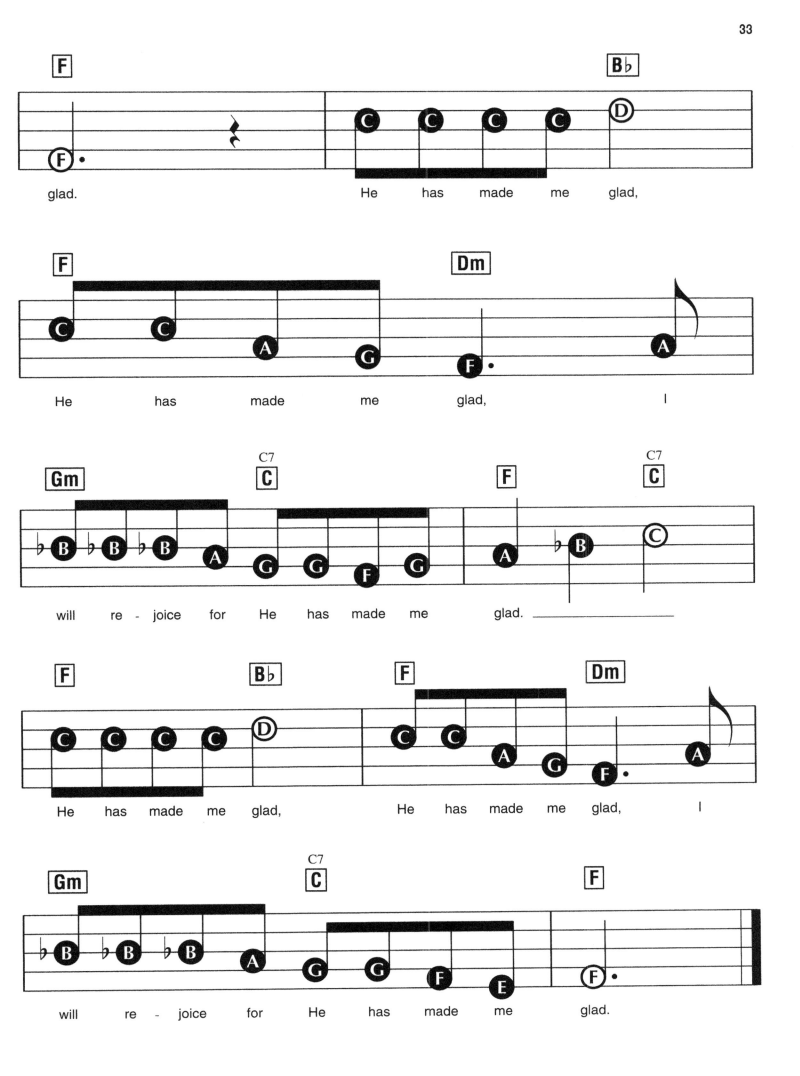

He Is Lord

Registration 1
Rhythm: Ballad

Text from Philippians 2:9-11
Traditional Music

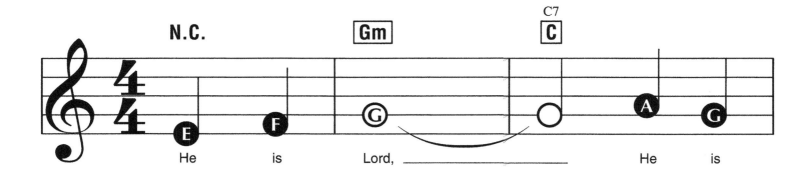

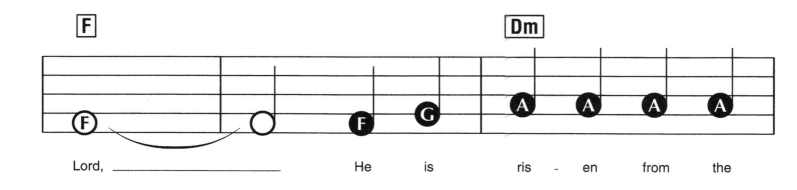

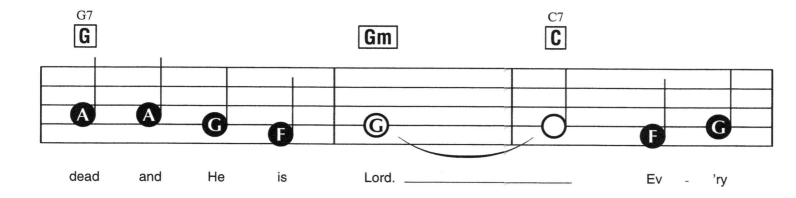

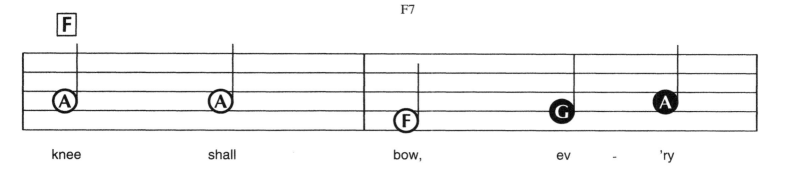

knee   shall   bow,   ev -   'ry

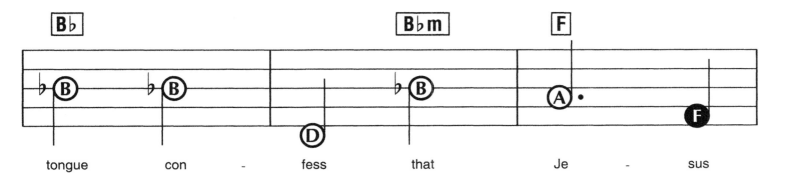

tongue   con -   fess   that   Je -   sus

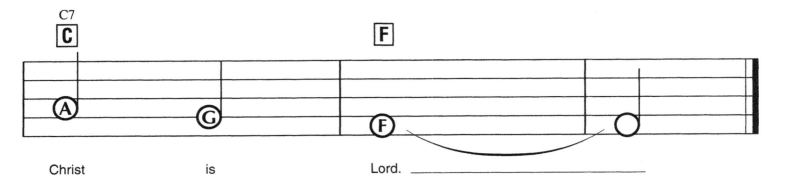

Christ   is   Lord.

How Majestic Is Your Name

Registration 5
Rhythm: Rock

Words and Music by
Michael W. Smith

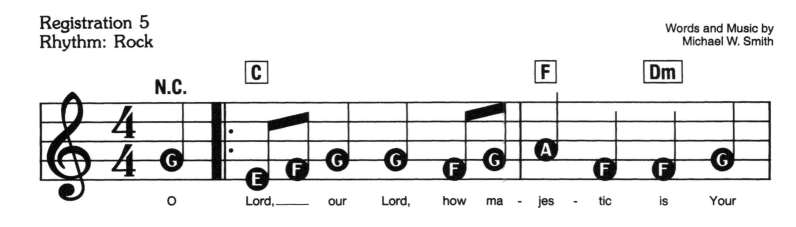

O Lord, our Lord, how ma - jes - tic is Your

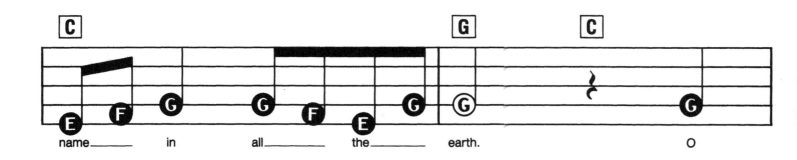

name in all the earth. O

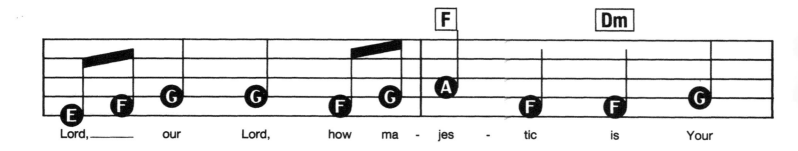

Lord, our Lord, how ma - jes - tic is Your

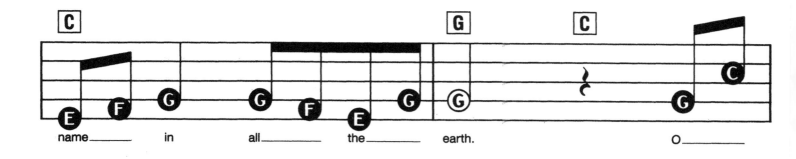

name in all the earth. O

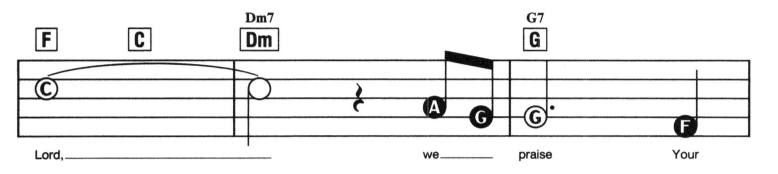

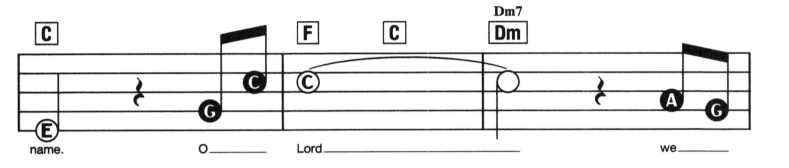

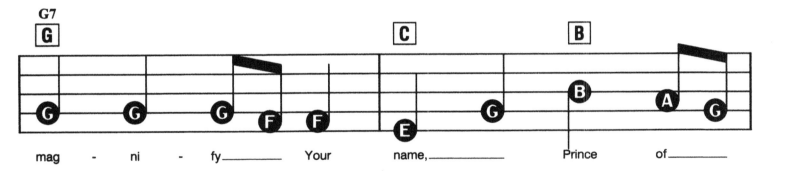

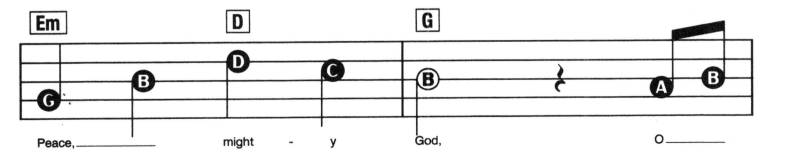

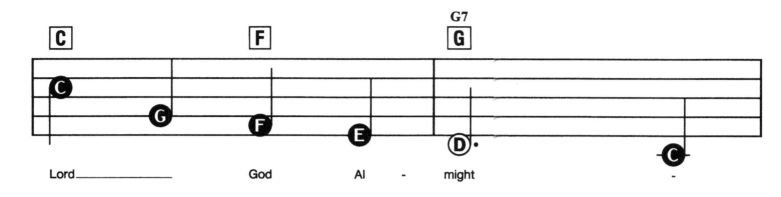

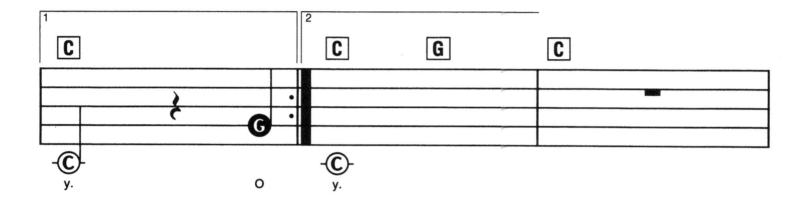

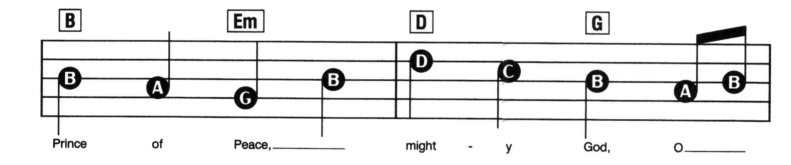

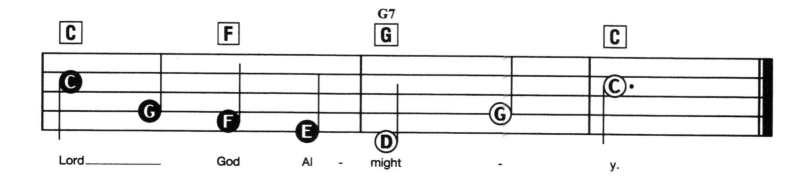

Jesus Is Lord of All

Registration 3
Rhythm: Ballad or 8 Beat

Words and Music by Ernie Rettino
and Debbie Kerner-Rettino

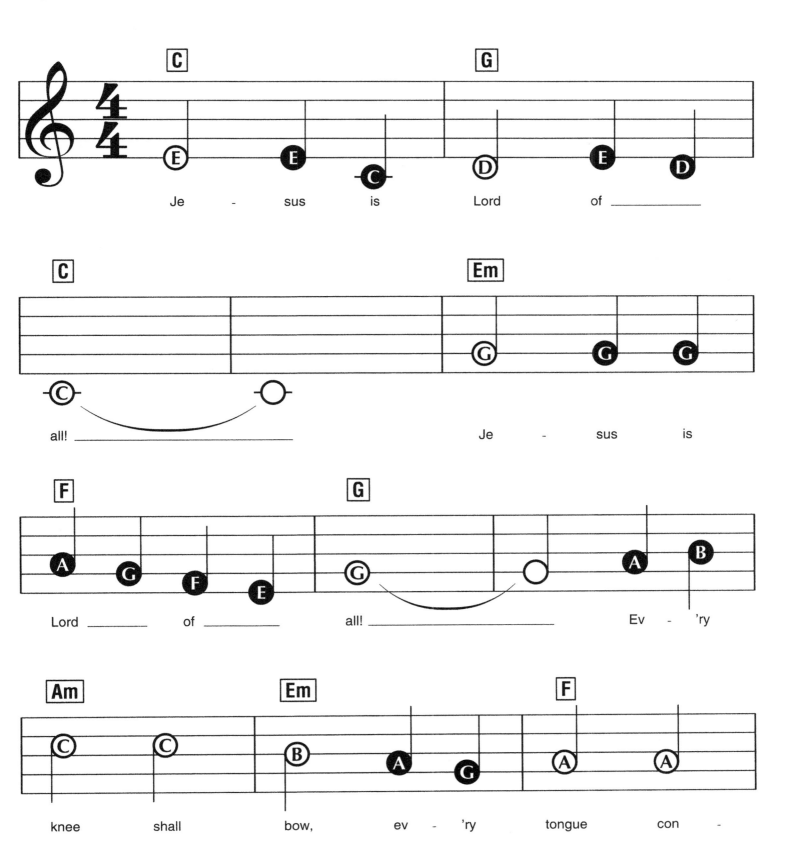

To Coda ⊕

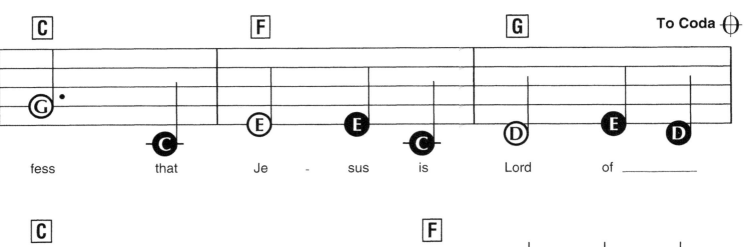

fess   that   Je - sus   is   Lord   of _____

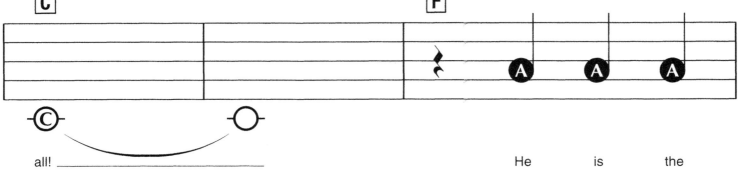

all! _____   He   is   the

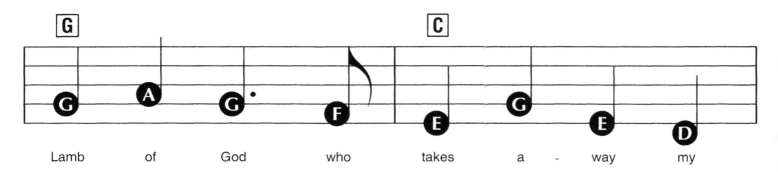

Lamb   of   God   who   takes   a - way   my

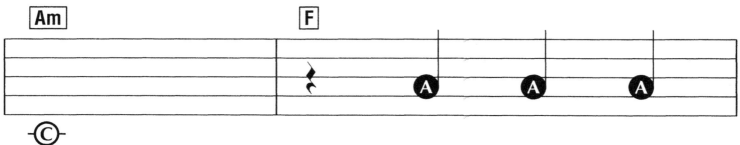

sin.   He   is   the

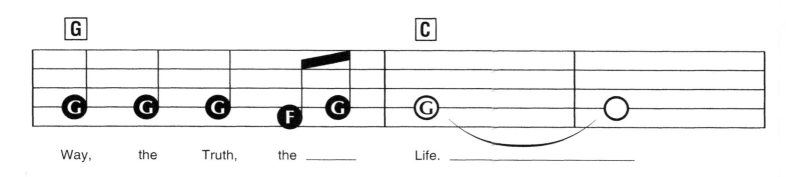

Way,   the   Truth,   the _____   Life. _____

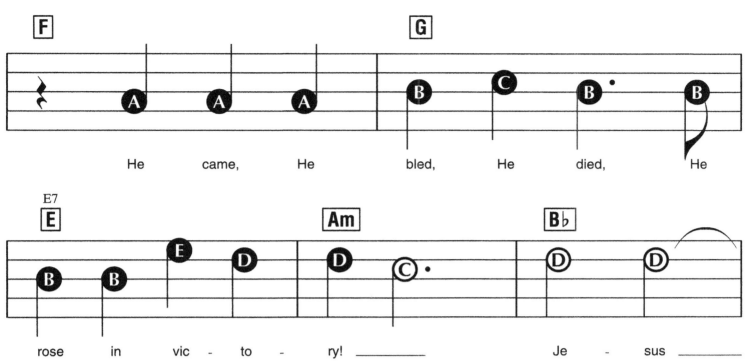

He came, He bled, He died, He

rose in vic - to - ry! _____ Je - sus _____

D.C. al Coda
(Return to beginning
Play to ⊕ and
Skip to Coda)

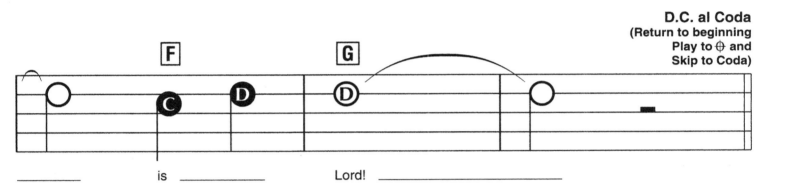

_____ is _____ Lord! _____

CODA

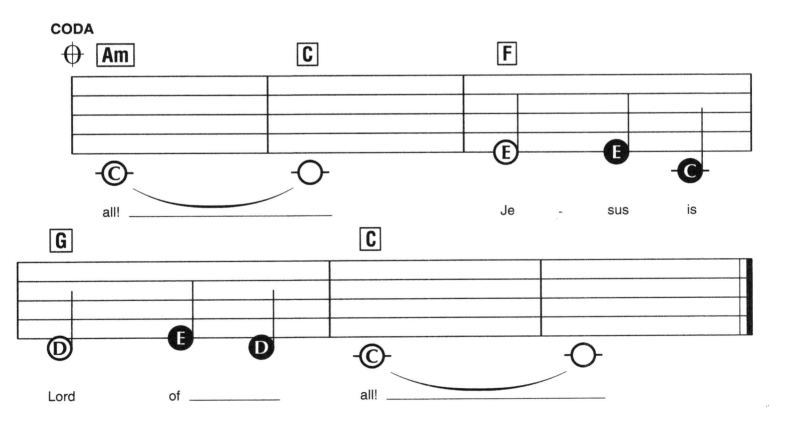

all! _____ Je - sus is

Lord of _____ all! _____

I Love You Lord

Registration 6
Rhythm: Ballad

Words and Music by
Laurie Klein

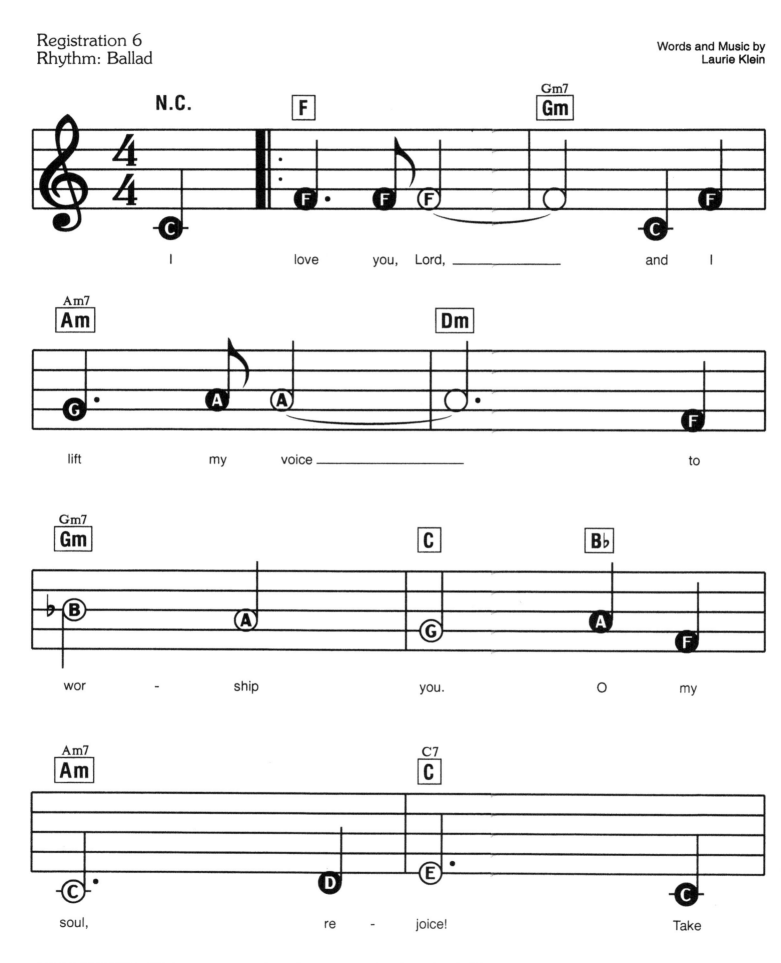

43

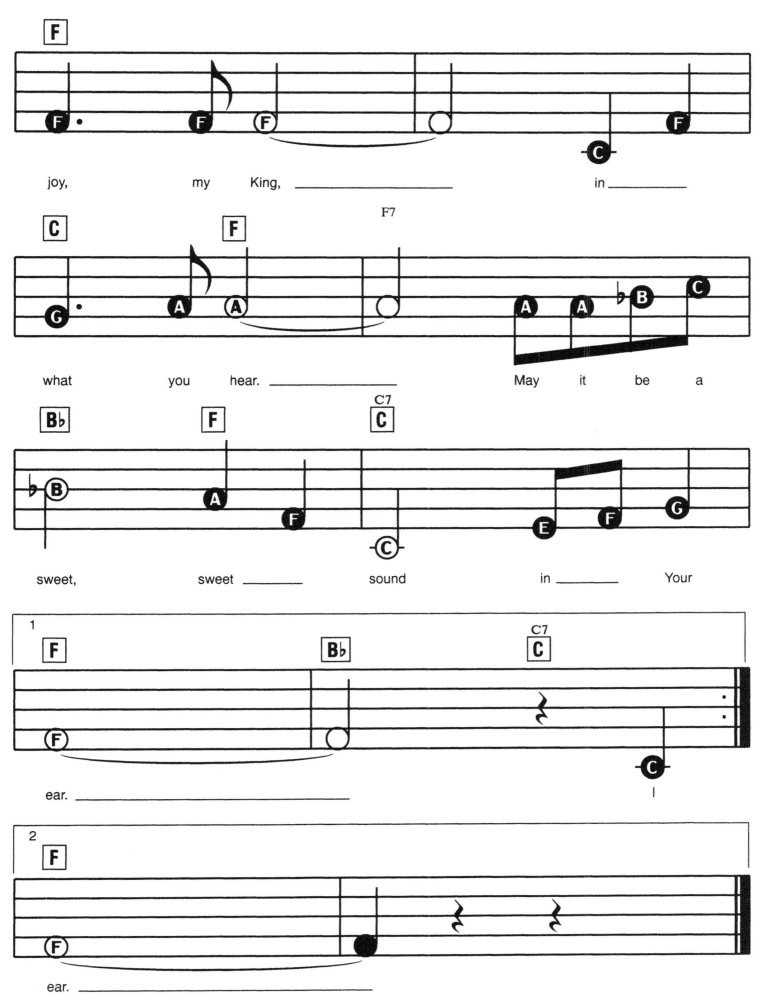

I Will Sing of the Mercies

Registration 7
Rhythm: March or Gospel

Words based on Psalm 89:1
Music by James H. Fillmore

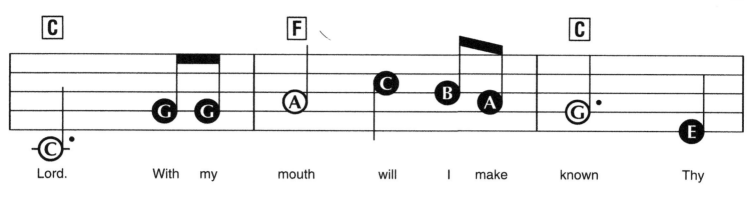

Lord.   With   my   mouth   will   I   make   known   Thy

faith – ful – ness,   Thy   faith – ful – ness.   With   my   mouth   will   I   make

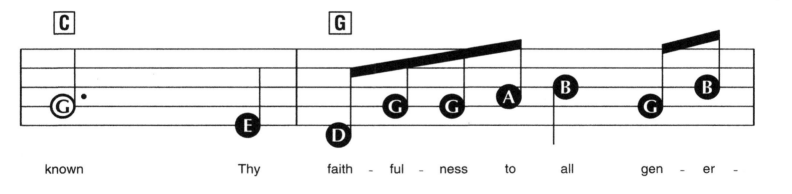

known   Thy   faith – ful – ness   to   all   gen – er –

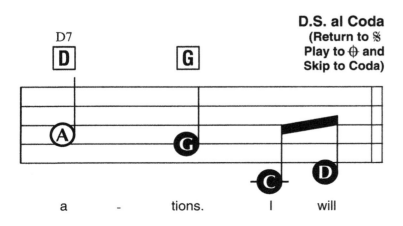

a –   tions.   I   will

D.S. al Coda
(Return to %
Play to ⊕ and
Skip to Coda)

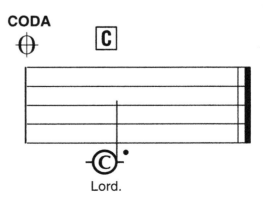

CODA

Lord.

Jesus, Name Above All Names

Registration 1
Rhythm: Waltz

Words and Music by
Naida Hearn

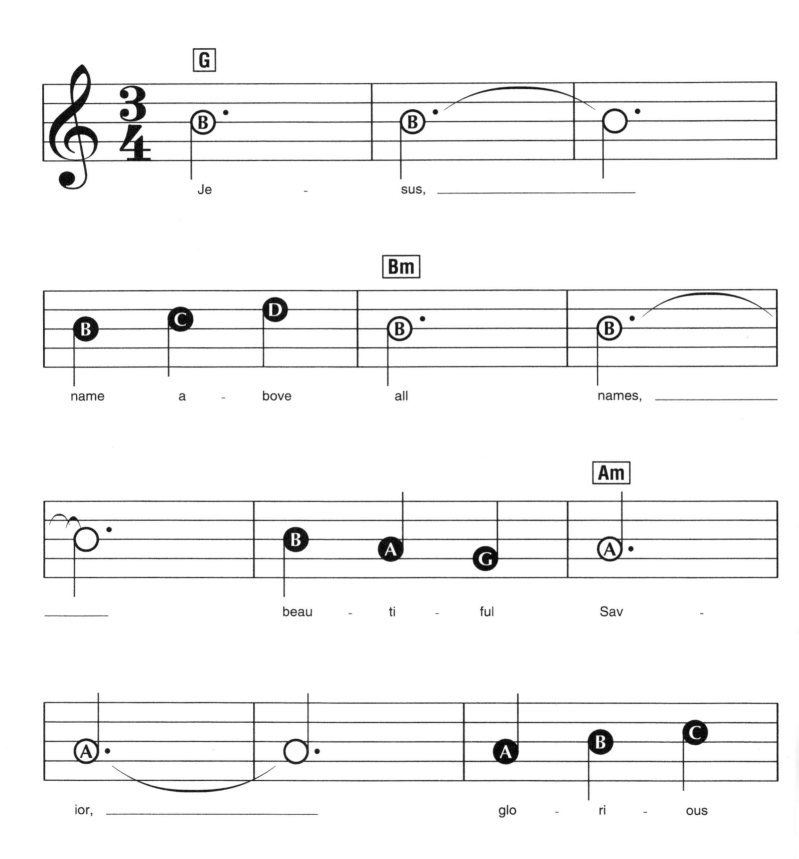

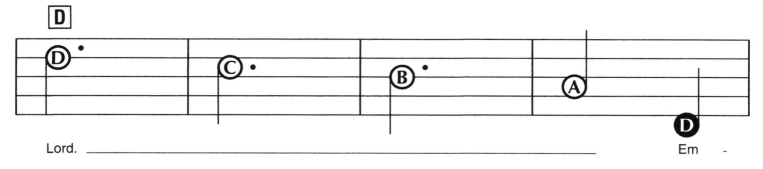

Lord. _____ Em -

man - u - el, _____ God _____ is

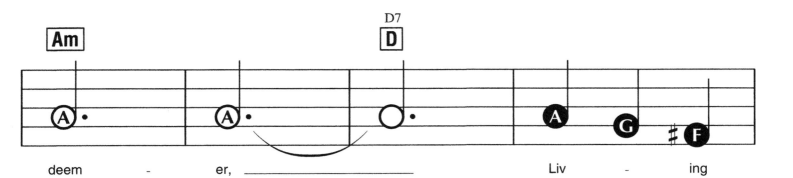

with us, _____ bless - ed Re -

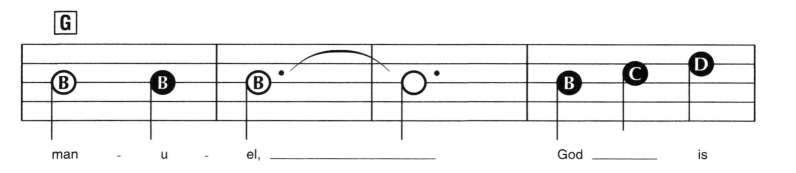

deem - er, _____ Liv - ing

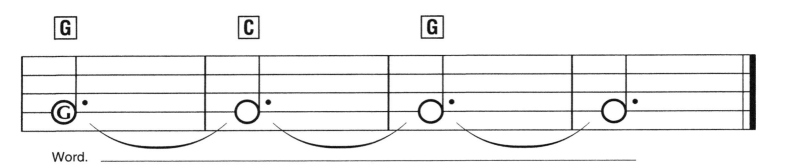

Word. _____

Lamb of God

Registration 1
Rhythm: Waltz

Words and Music by
Twila Paris

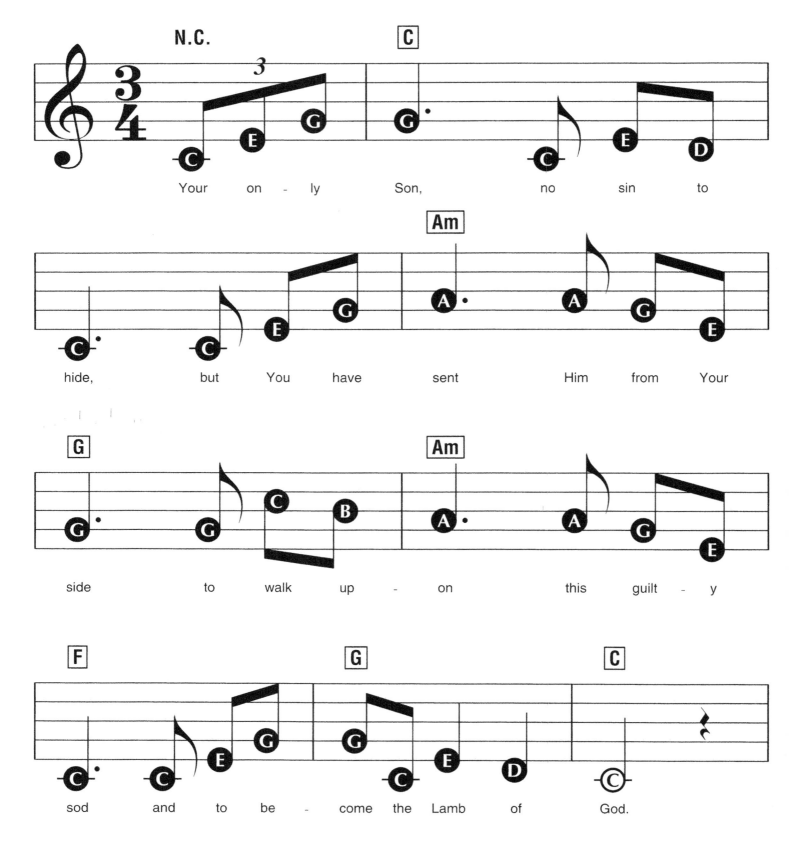

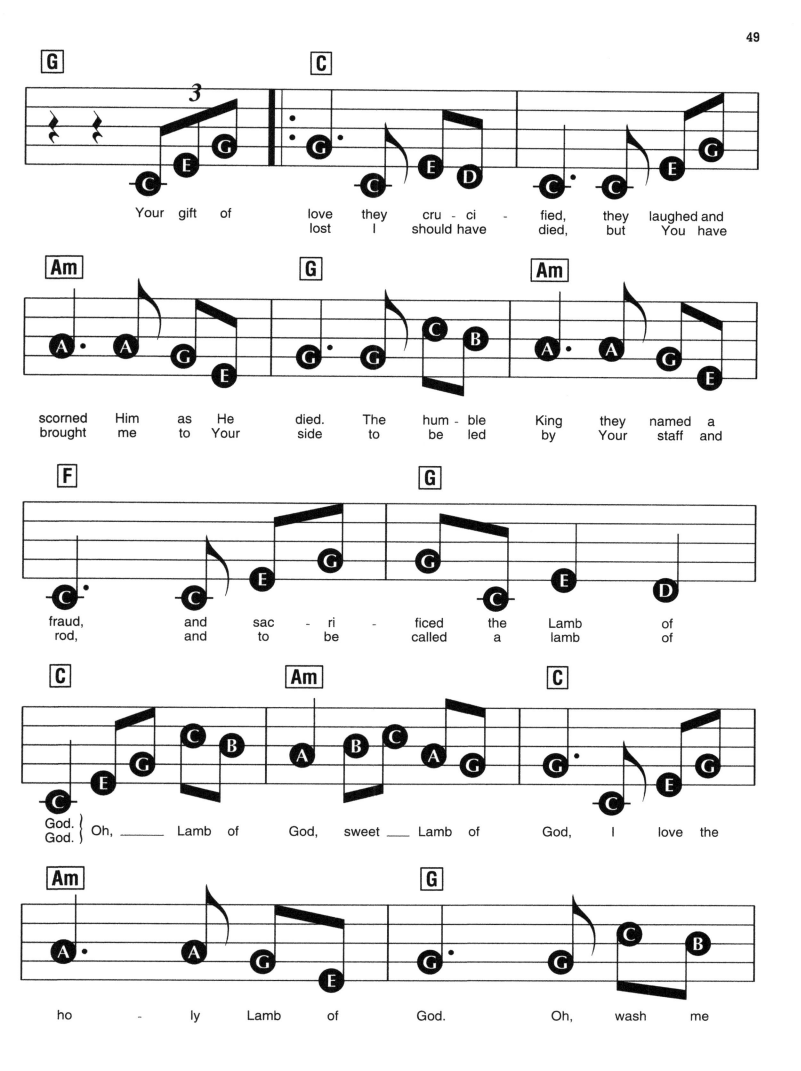

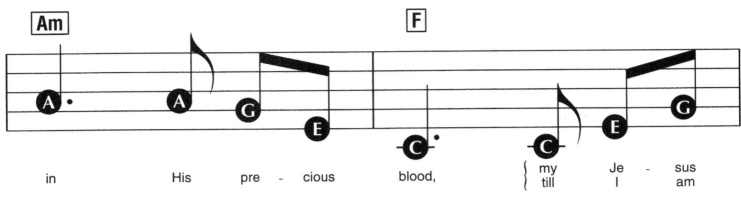

in His pre - cious blood, { my Je - sus
{ till I am

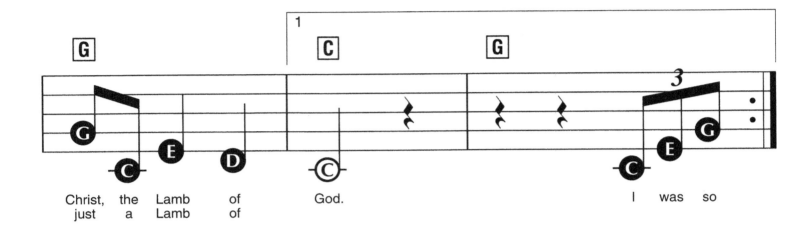

Christ, the Lamb of God. I was so
just a Lamb of

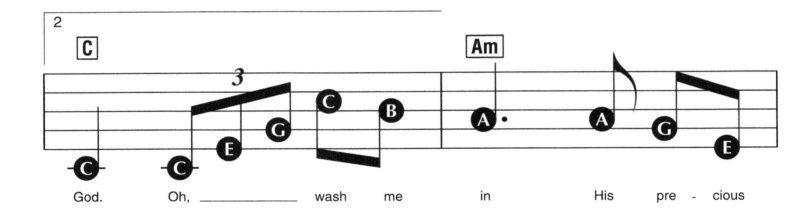

God. Oh, _____ wash me in His pre - cious

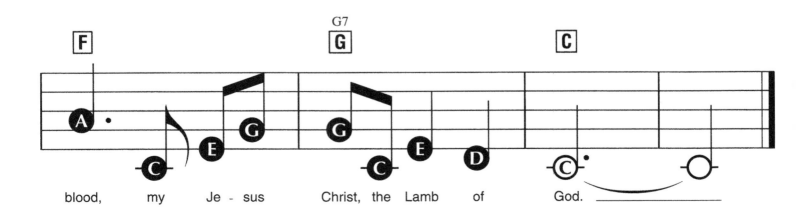

blood, my Je - sus Christ, the Lamb of God. _____

Shine, Jesus, Shine

Registration 2
Rhythm: 16 Beat or Disco

Words and Music by
Graham Kendrick

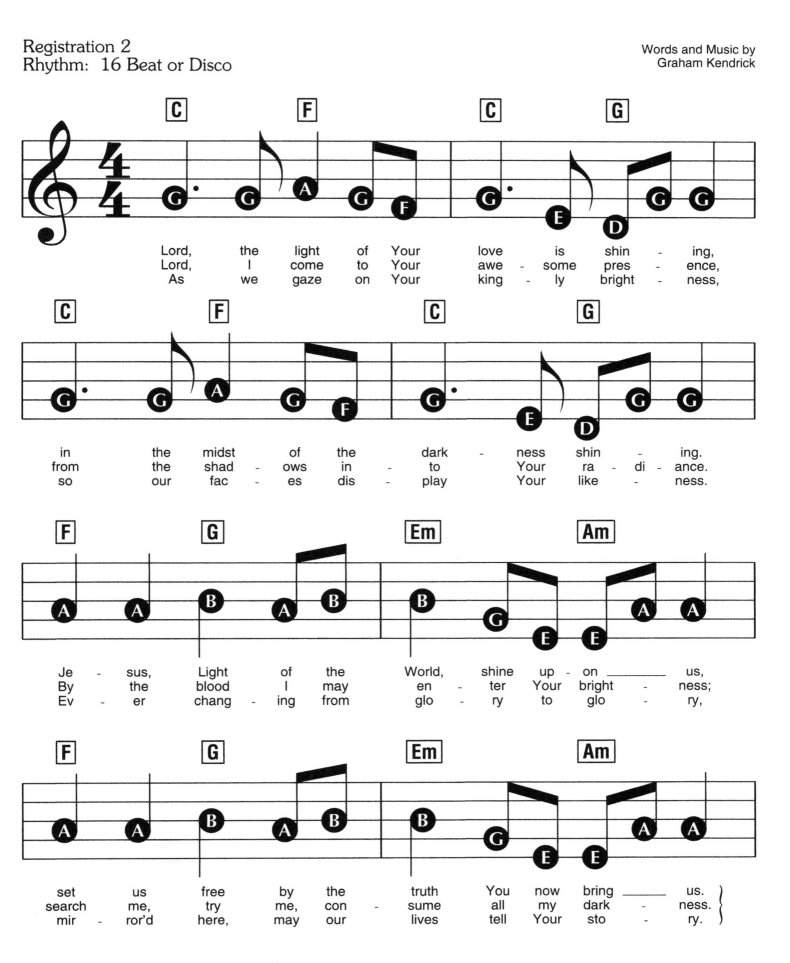

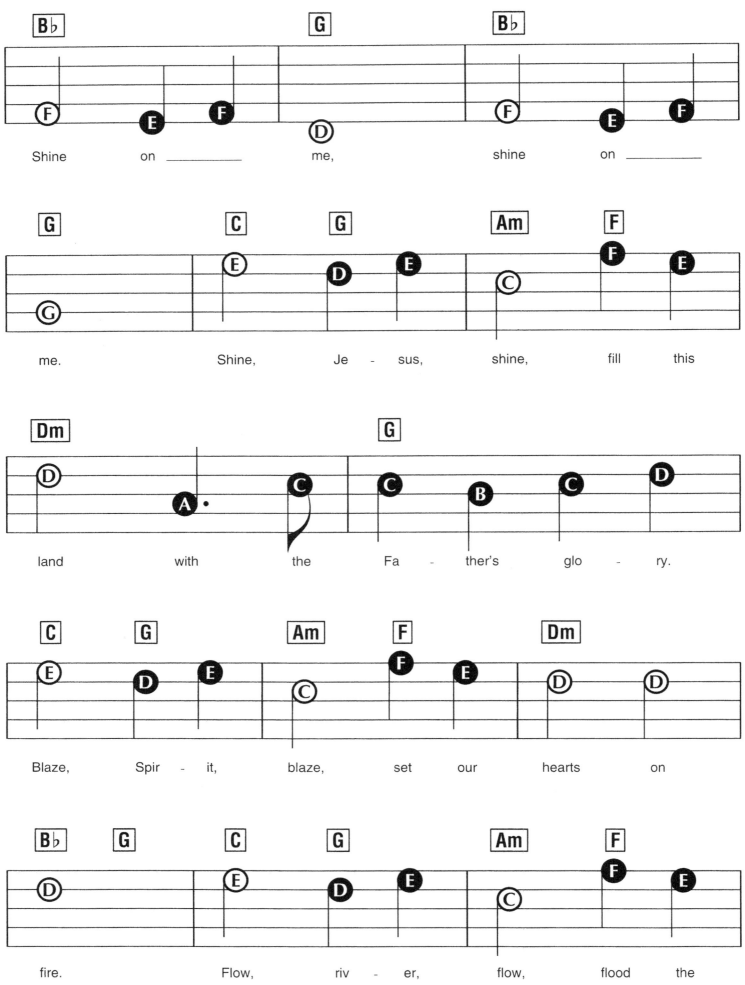

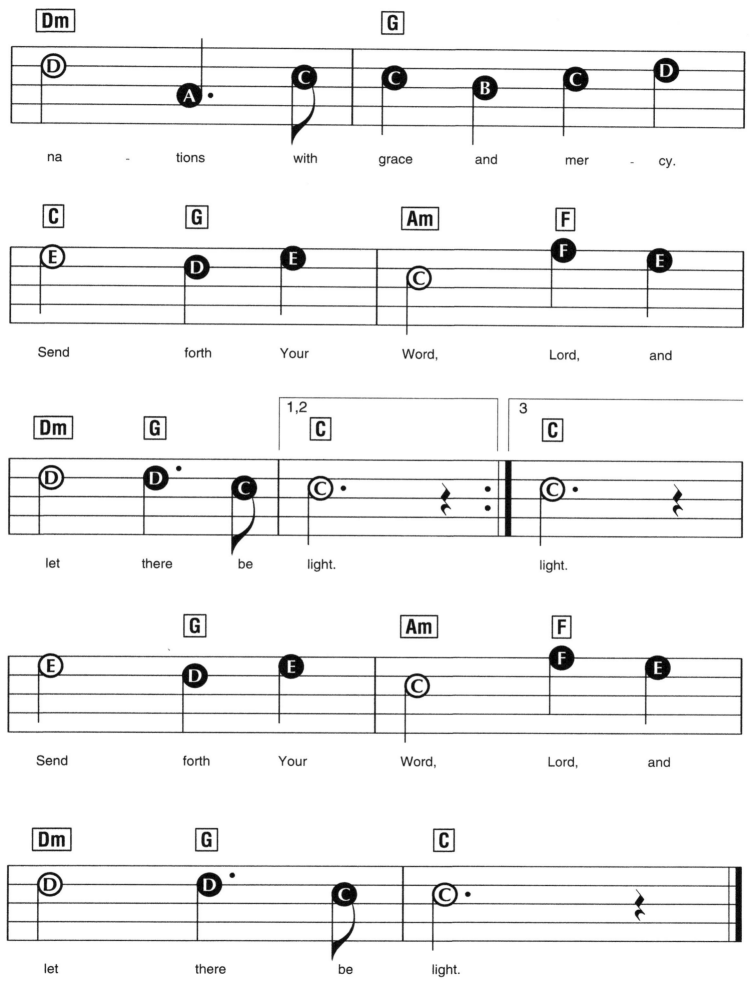

Lord, I Lift Your Name on High

Registration 7
Rhythm: Pop or 16 Beat

Words and Music by
Rick Founds

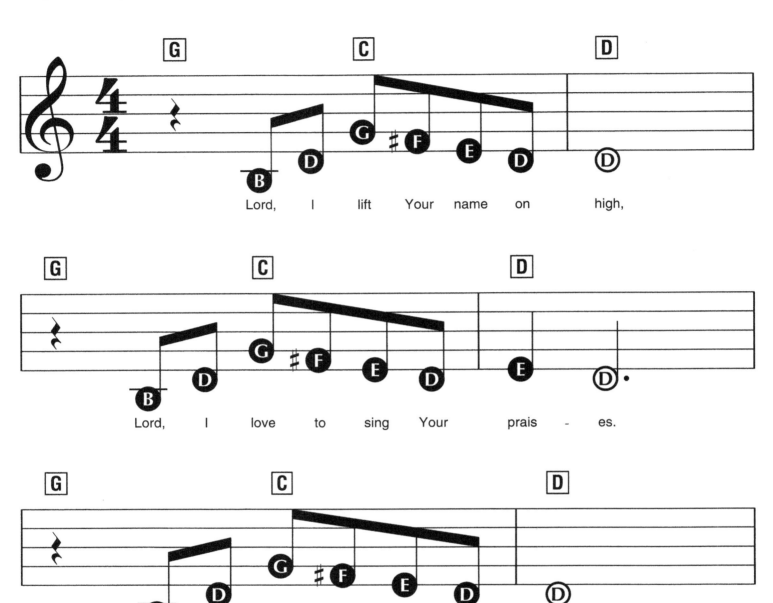

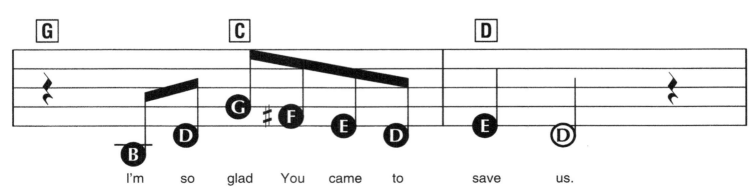

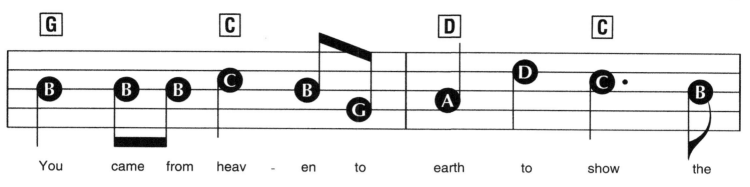

You came from heav - en to earth to show the

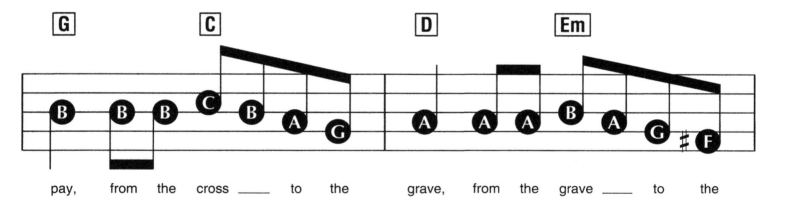

way, from the earth ____ to the cross, my debt to

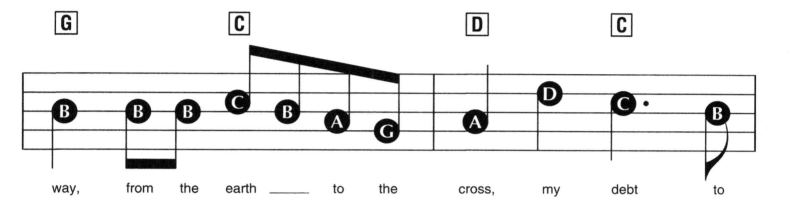

pay, from the cross ____ to the grave, from the grave ____ to the

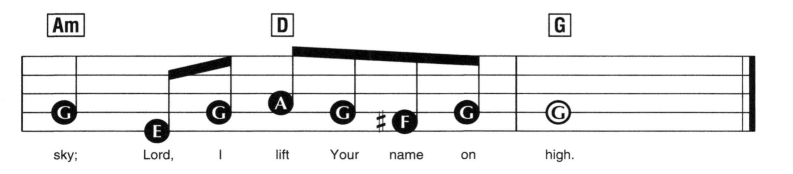

sky; Lord, I lift Your name on high.

More Precious Than Silver

Registration 1
Rhythm: Ballad

Words and Music by
Lynn DeShazo

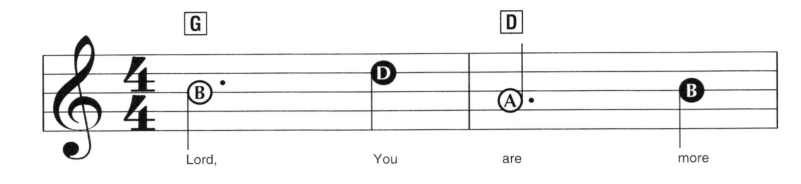

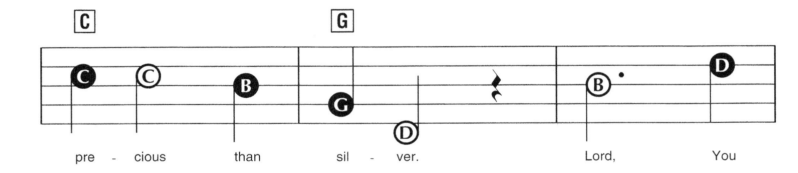

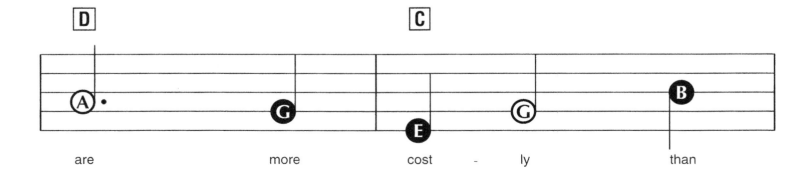

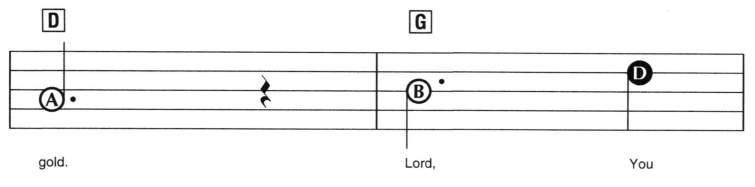

gold.   Lord,   You

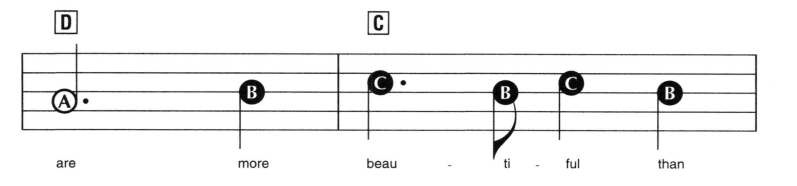

are   more   beau - ti - ful than

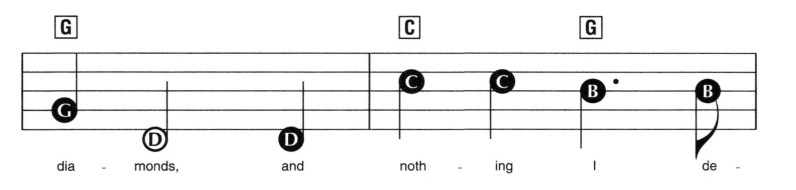

dia - monds,   and   noth - ing   I   de -

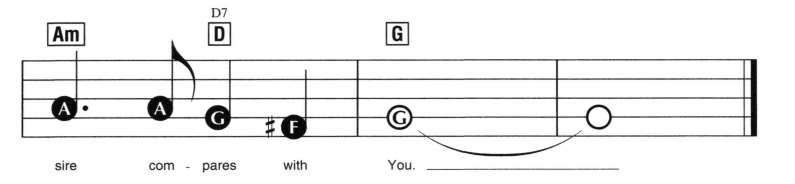

sire   com - pares   with   You.

O How He Loves You and Me

Registration 8
Rhythm: Waltz

Words and Music by
Kurt Kaiser

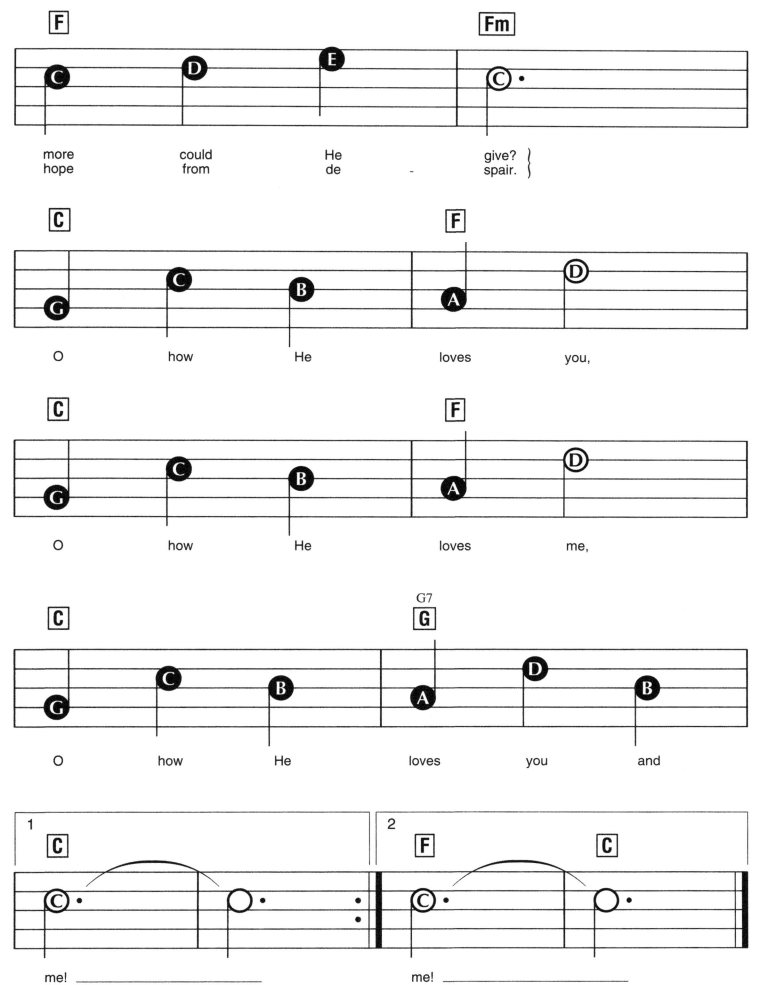

Oh Lord, You're Beautiful

Registration 4
Rhythm: Rock or Gospel

Words and Music by
Keith Green

61

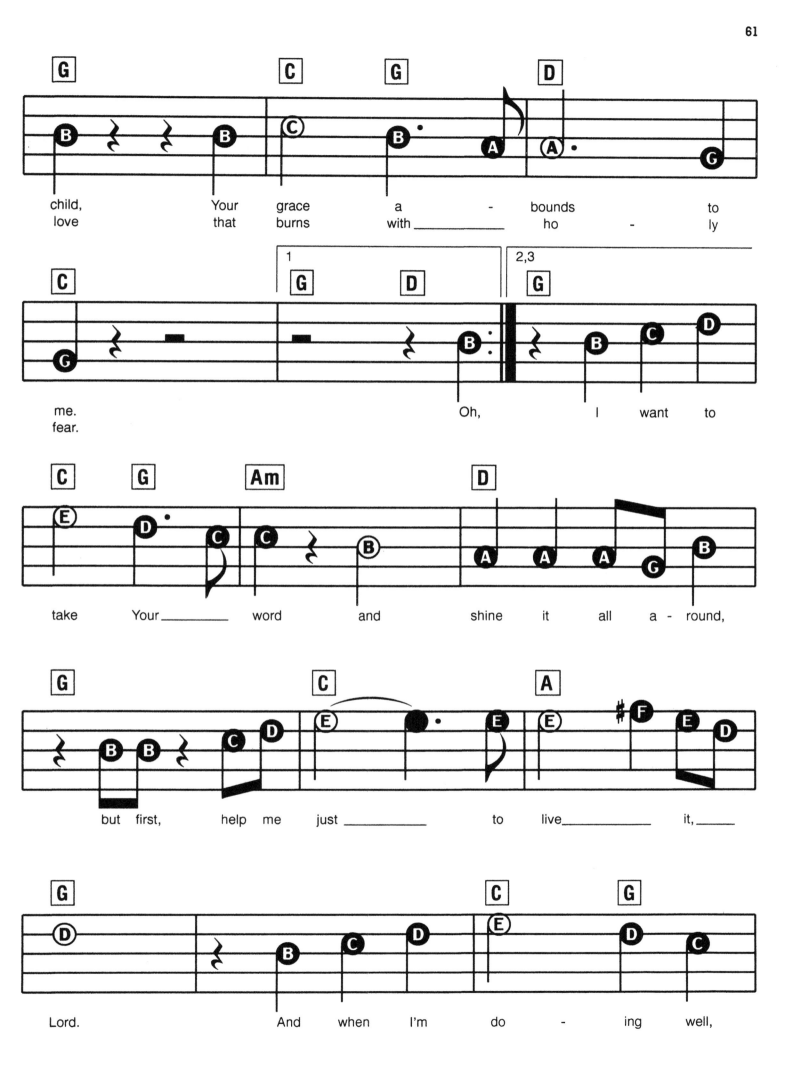

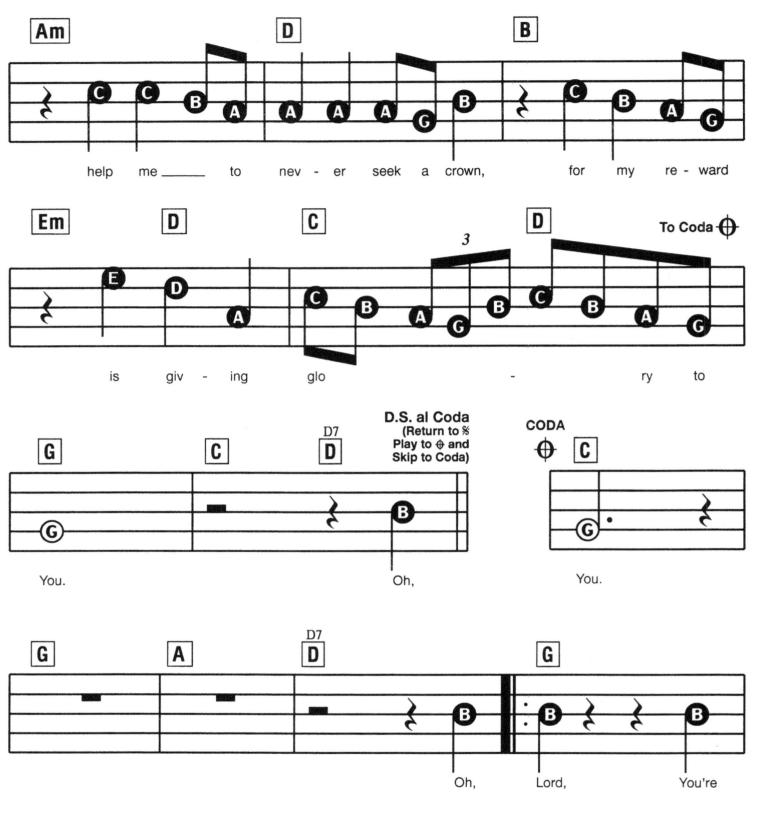

help me _____ to nev - er seek a crown, for my re - ward

is giv - ing glo - ry to

D.S. al Coda
(Return to 𝄋
Play to ⊕ and
Skip to Coda)

CODA

You. Oh, You.

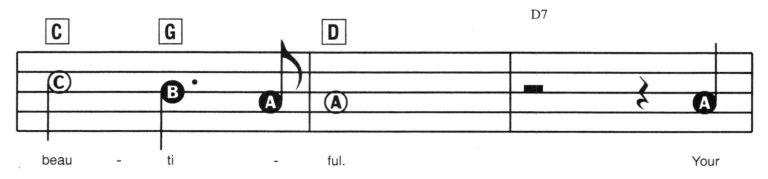

Oh, Lord, You're

beau - ti - ful. Your

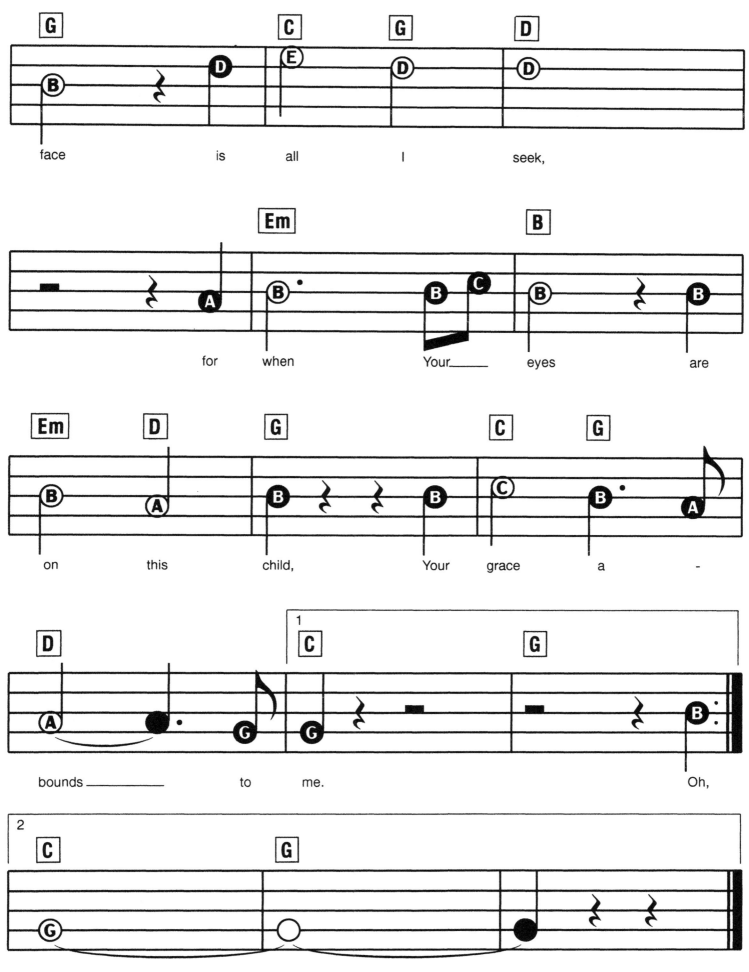

Open Our Eyes

Registration 3
Rhythm: Waltz

Words and Music by
Bob Cull

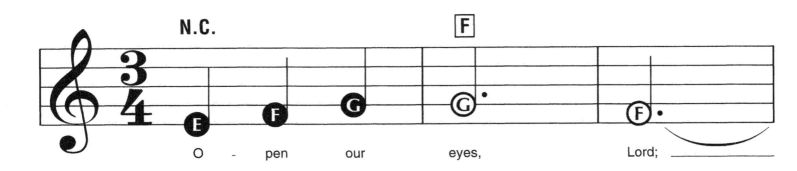

O - pen our eyes, Lord; _____

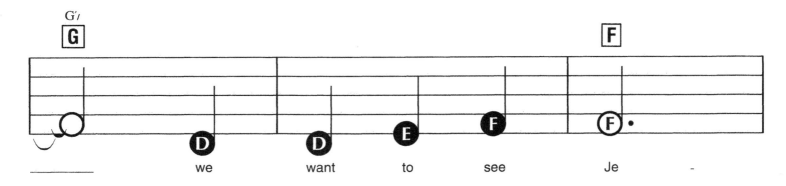

_____ we want to see Je -

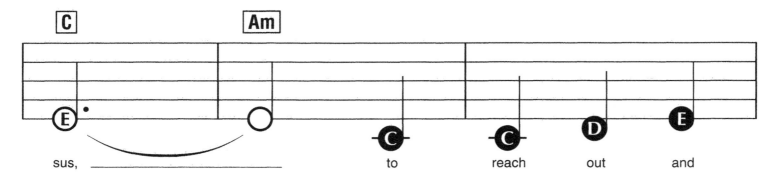

sus, _____ to reach out and

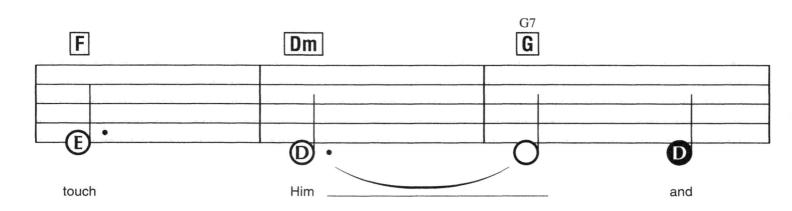

touch Him _____ and

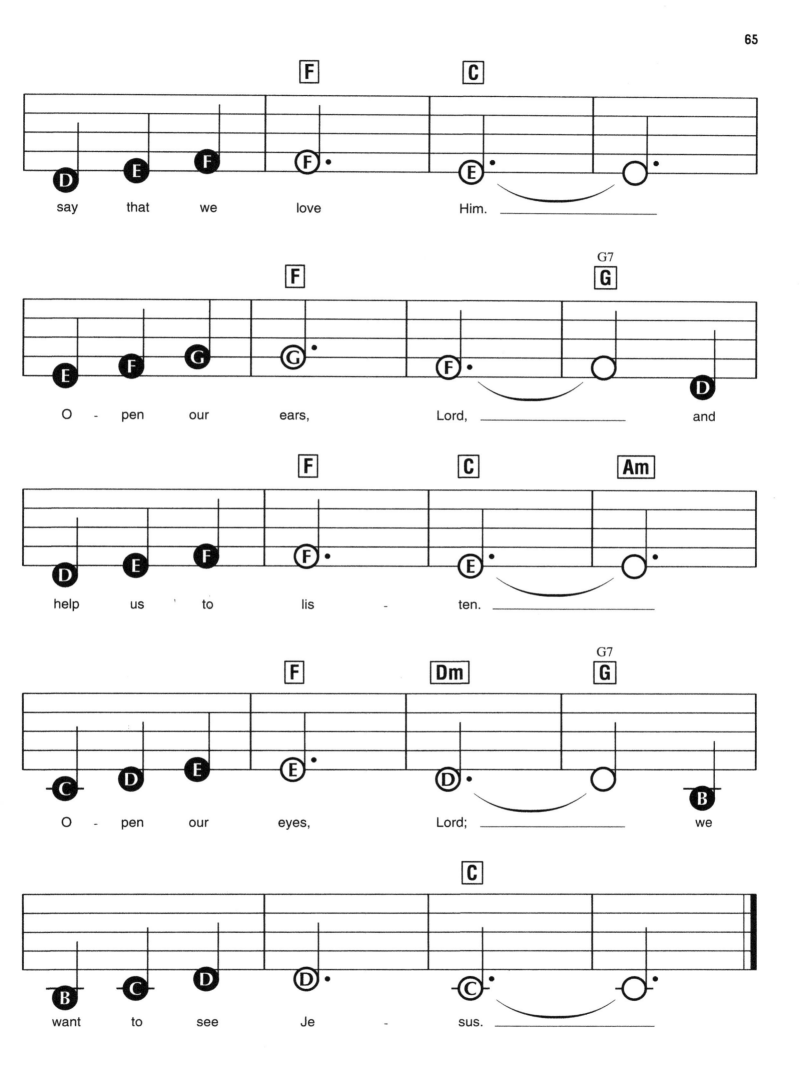

The Power of Your Love

Registration 8
Rhythm: Ballad or 8 Beat

Words and Music by
Geoff Bullock

C **G** **Am**

E F G D C E E F G

Lord, I come to You; let my heart be
Lord, un - veil to my eyes; let me see You

Em **Am**

G D C C B B A

changed, re - newed, the flow - ing from the
face to face, the know - ledge of Your

F **G** **Am** **G**

A C E D G E

grace that I've found in You.
love as You live in me.

C **G** **Am**

E F G D C E E E F G

Lord, I've come to know the weak - ness - es I
Lord, re - new my mind as Your will un -

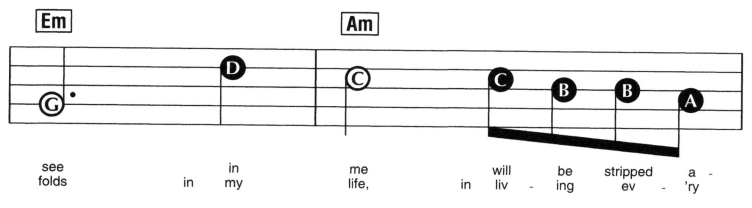

see folds in in my me life, will in liv be - stripped ing ev a - - 'ry

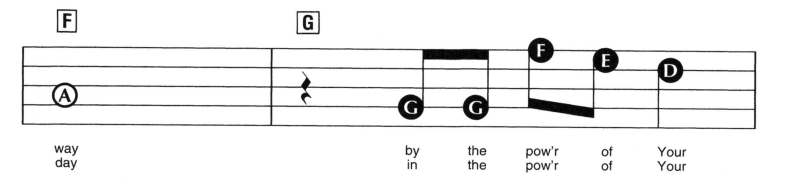

way day by in the the pow'r pow'r of of Your Your

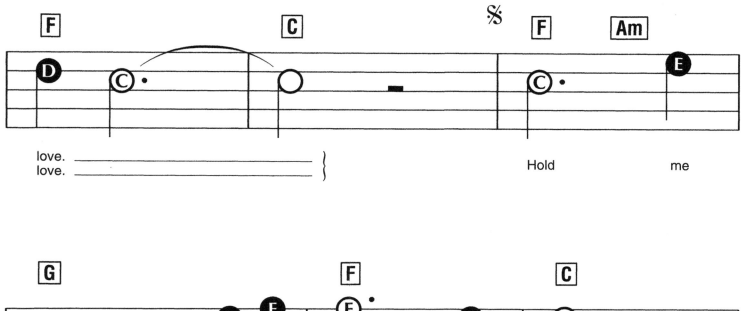

love.
love.

Hold me

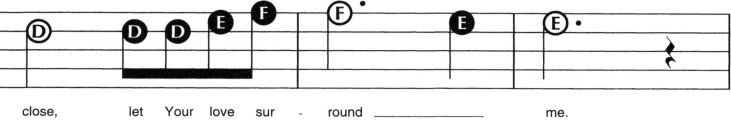

close, let Your love sur - round me.

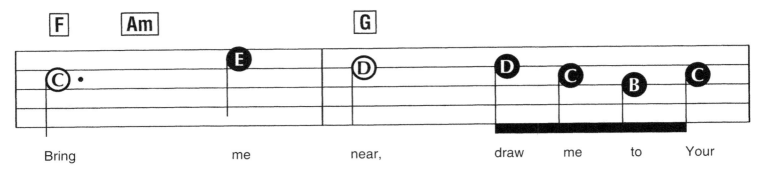

Bring me near, draw me to Your

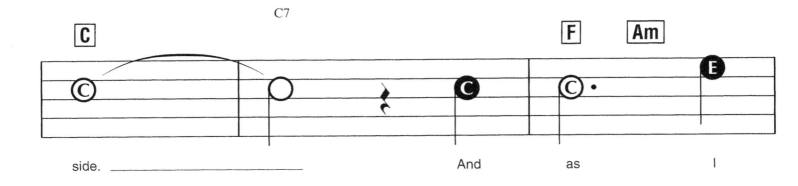

side. And as I

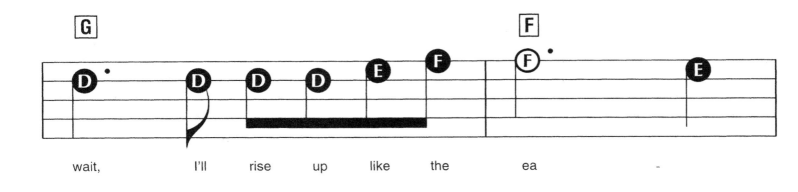

wait, I'll rise up like the ea -

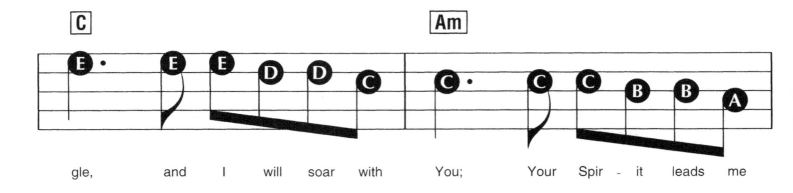

gle, and I will soar with You; Your Spir - it leads me

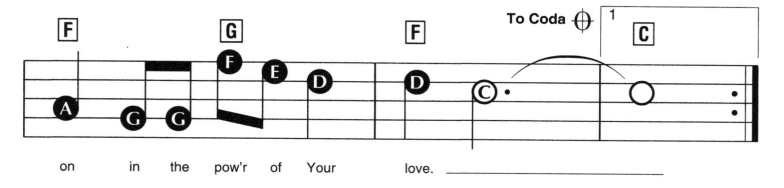

on   in   the   pow'r   of   Your   love. _____

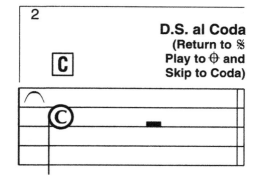

D.S. al Coda
(Return to %
Play to ⊕ and
Skip to Coda)

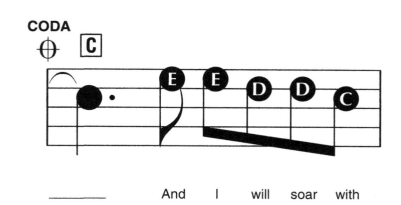

_____   And   I   will   soar   with

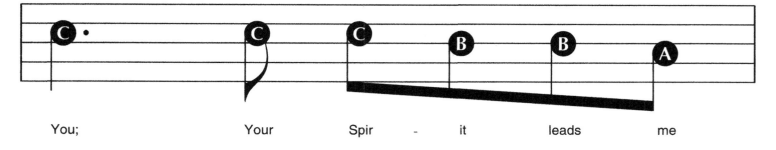

You;   Your   Spir - it   leads   me

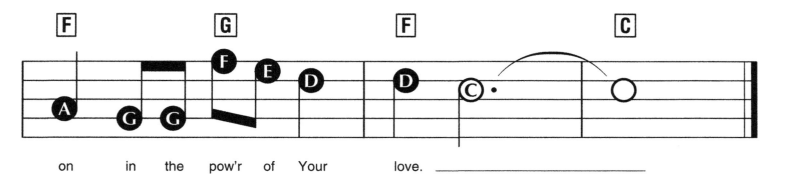

on   in   the   pow'r   of   Your   love. _____

Seek Ye First

Registration 1
Rhythm: Ballad

Words and Music by
Karen Lafferty

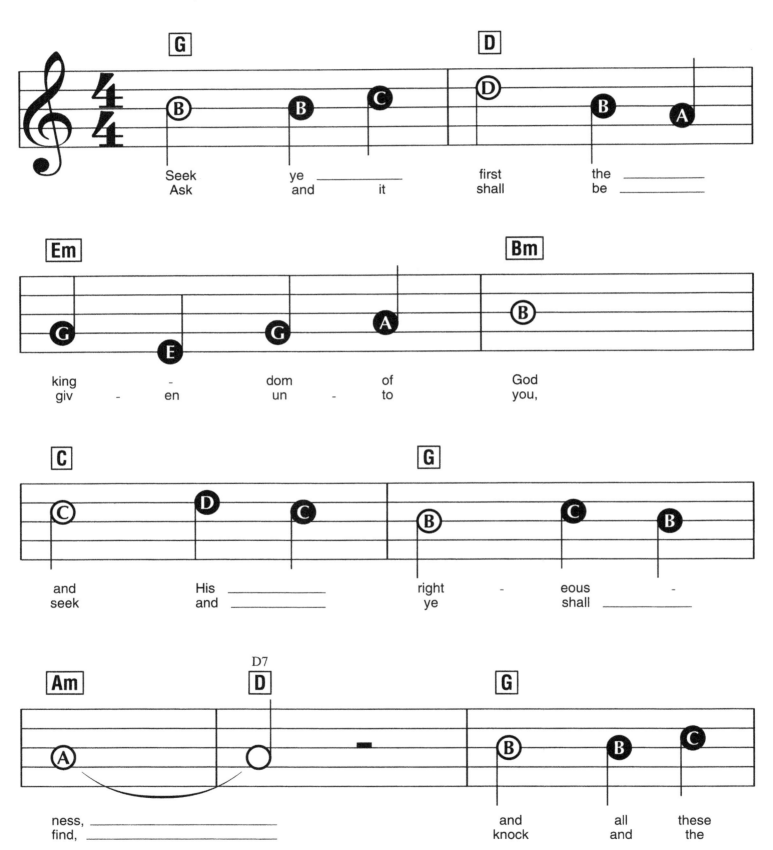

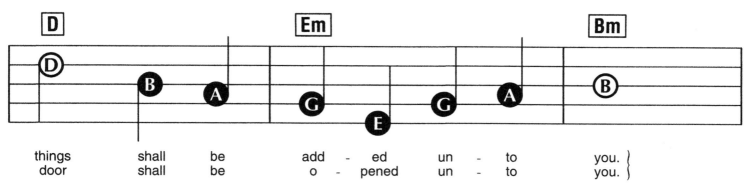

things   shall   be   add - ed   un - to   you. }
door   shall   be   o - pened   un - to   you. }

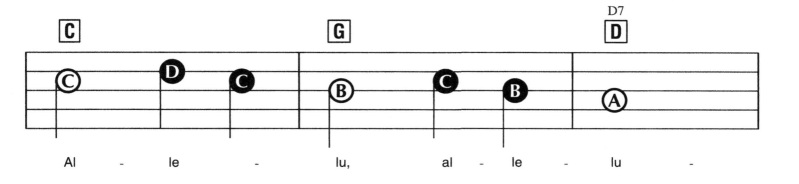

Al - le -   lu,   al - le - lu -

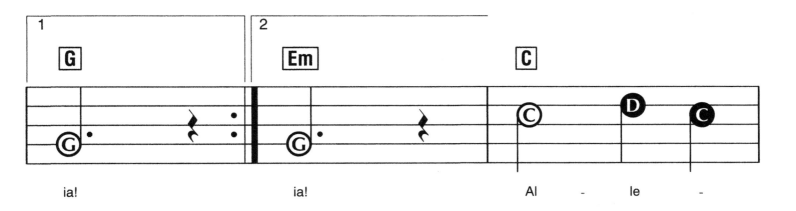

ia!   ia!   Al - le -

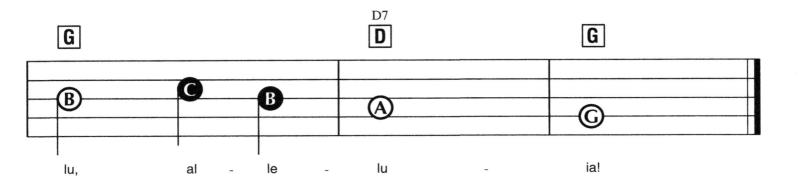

lu,   al - le - lu -   ia!

There Is a Redeemer

Registration 8
Rhythm: Ballad

Words and Music by
Melody Green

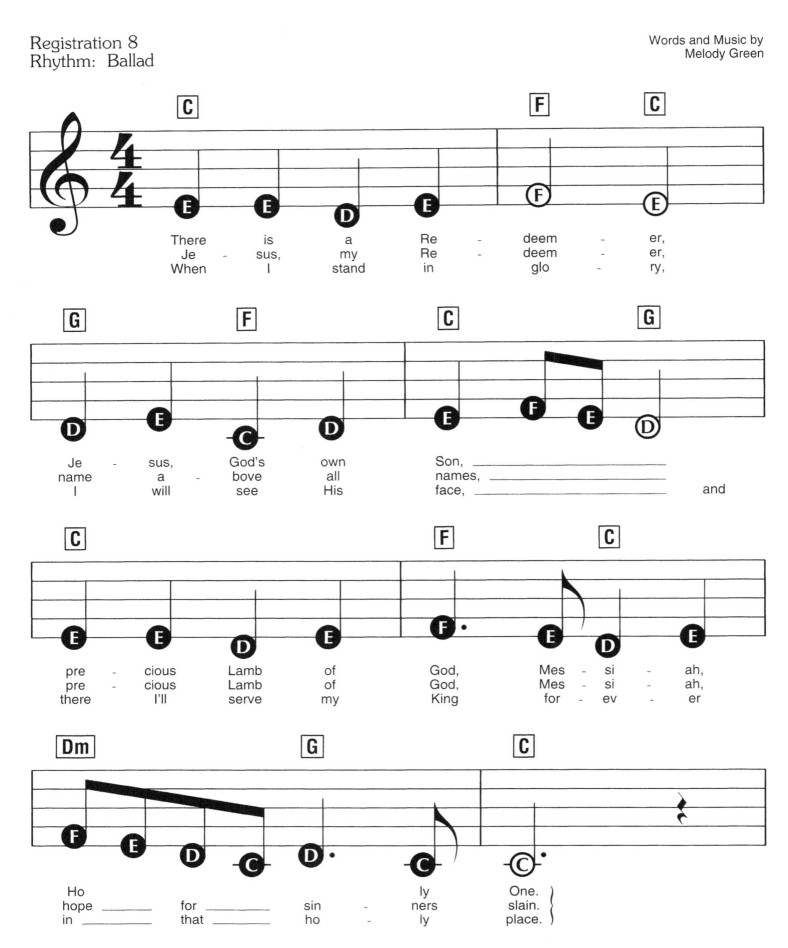

73

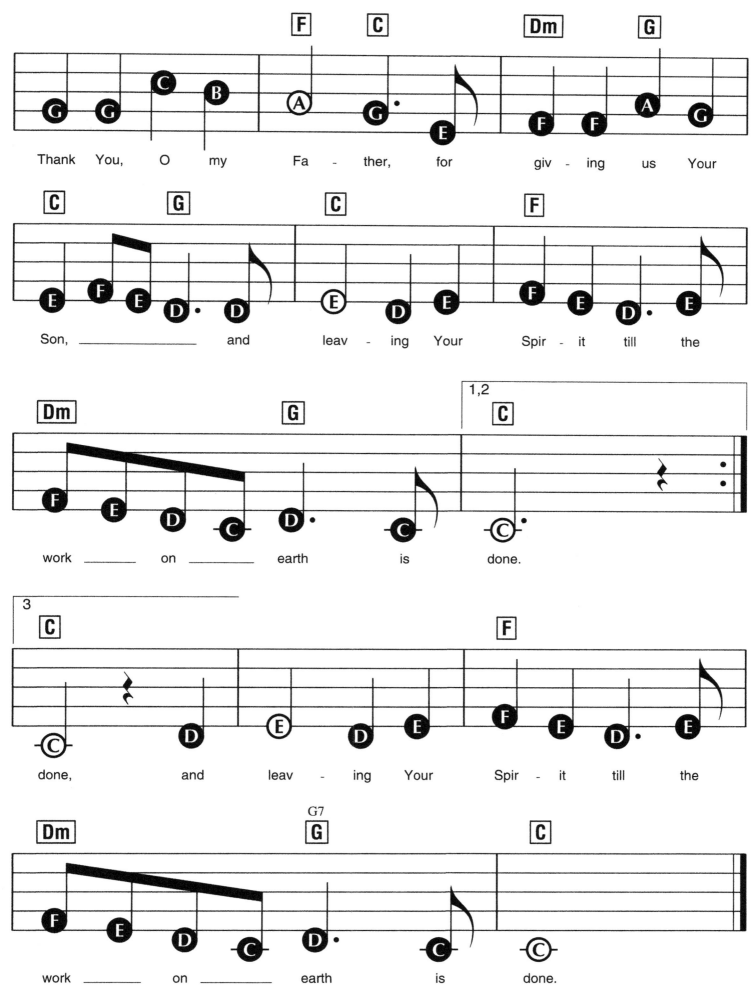

This Is the Day

Registration 9
Rhythm: Fox Trot

By Les Garrett

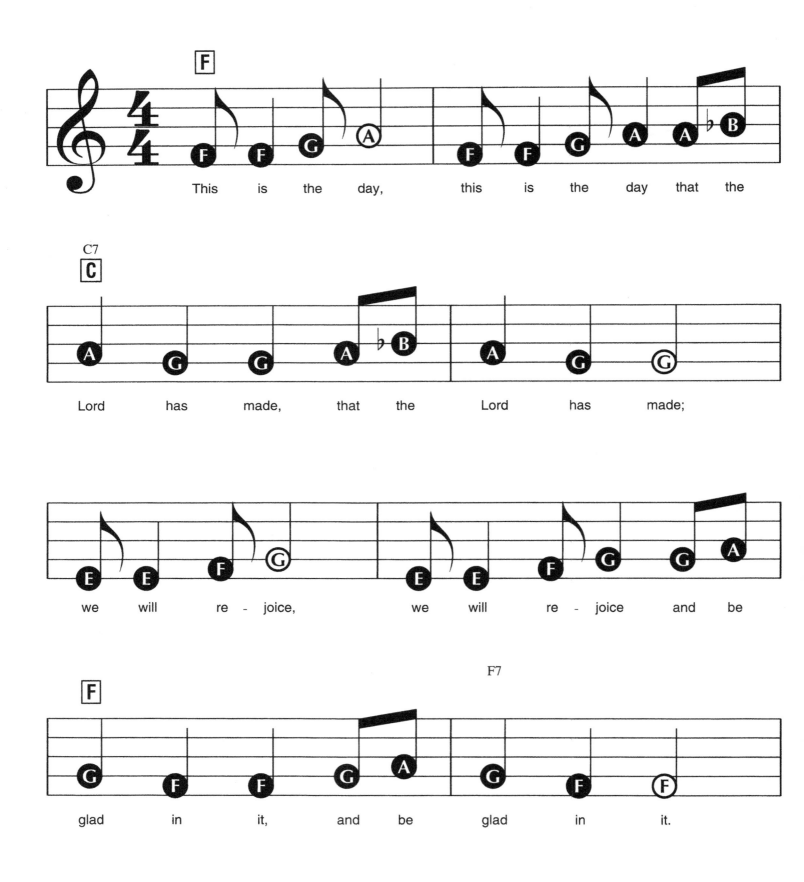

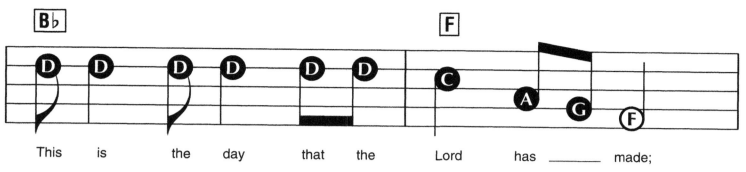

This is the day that the Lord has _____ made;

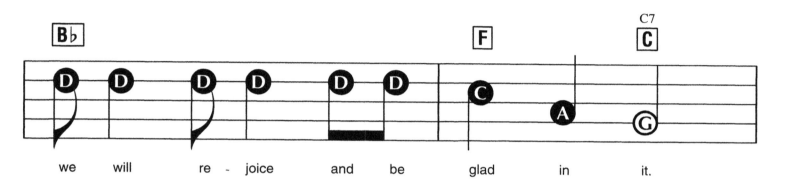

we will re - joice and be glad in it.

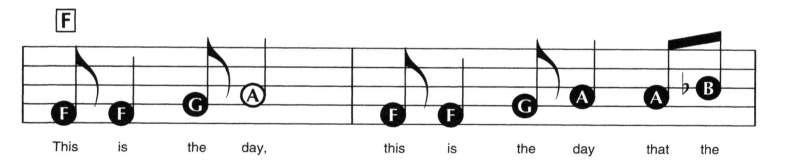

This is the day, this is the day that the

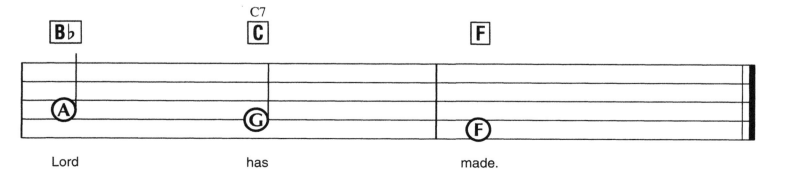

Lord has made.

We Will Glorify

Registration 4
Rhythm: Waltz

Words and Music by
Twila Paris

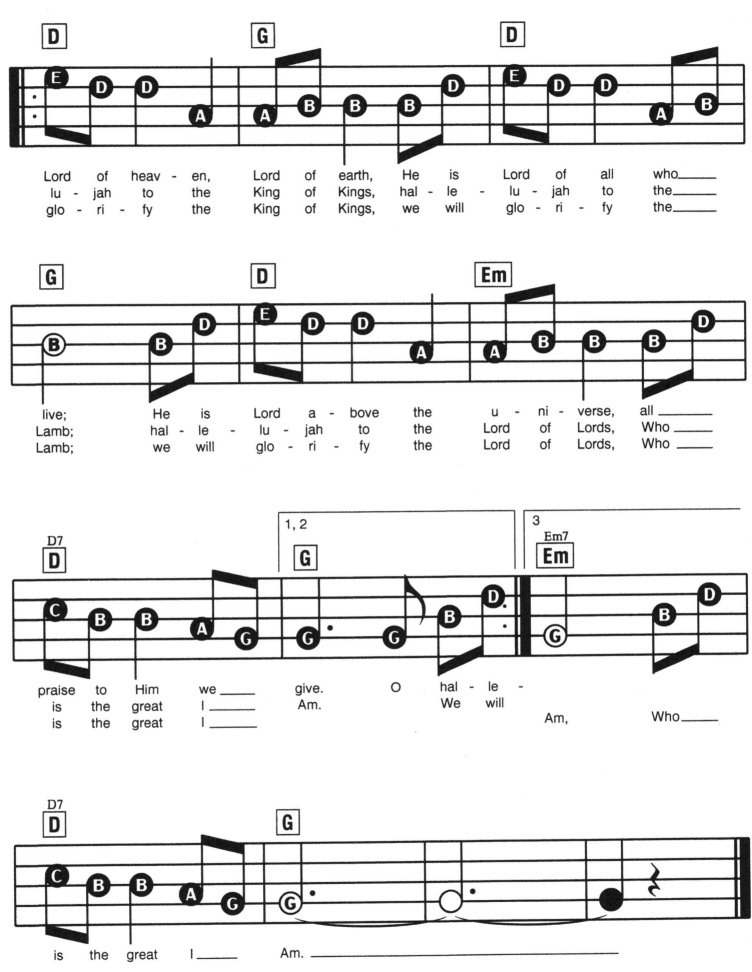

We Worship and Adore You

Registration 3
Rhythm: Ballad or 8 Beat

Traditional

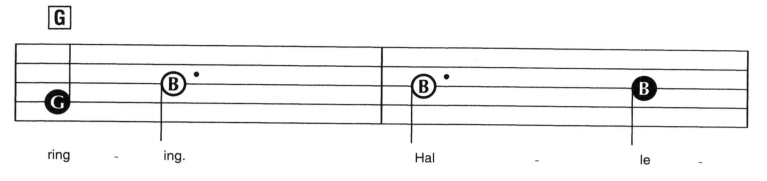

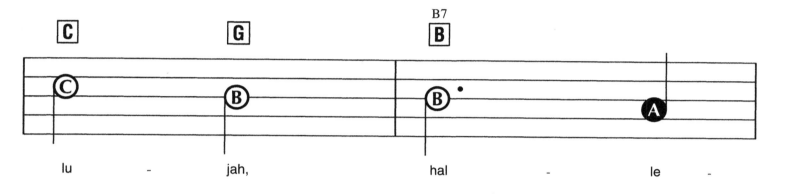

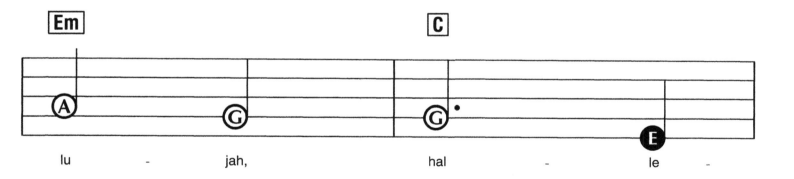

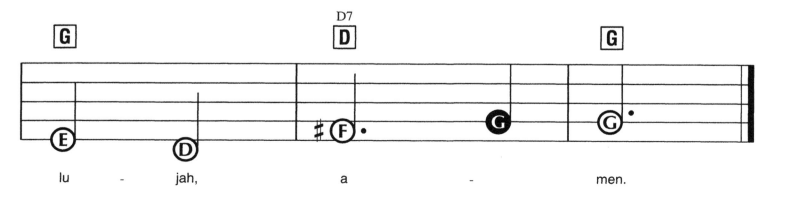

You Are My All in All

Registration 1
Rhythm: Ballad or 8 Beat

By Dennis Jernigan

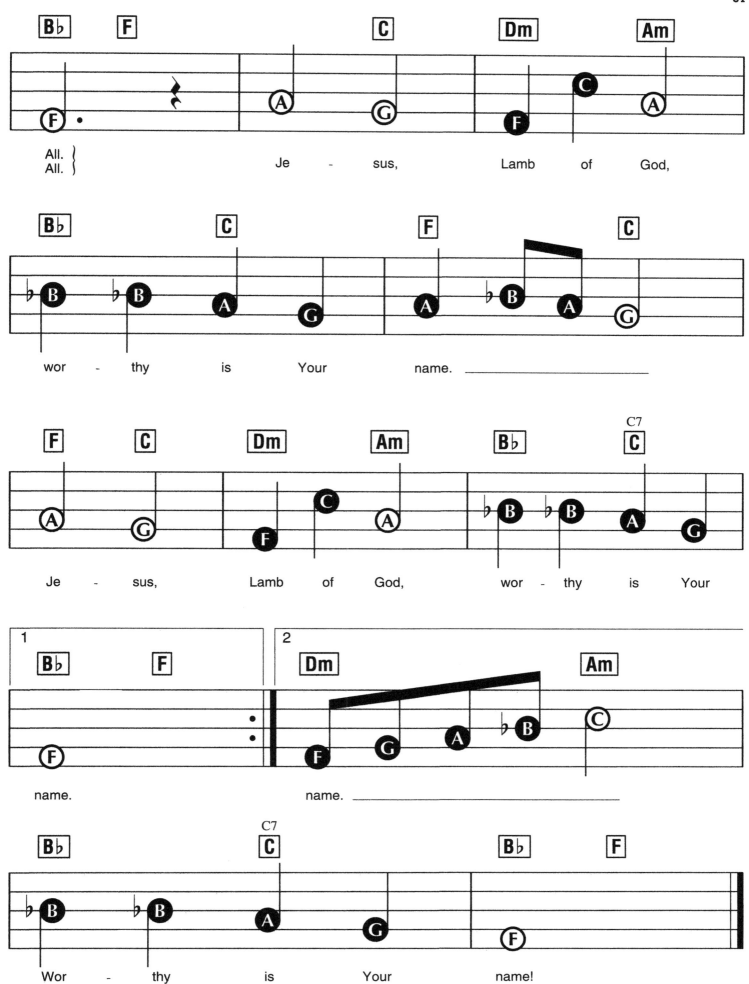

You Are My Hiding Place

Registration 1
Rhythm: Ballad

Words and Music by
Michael Ledner

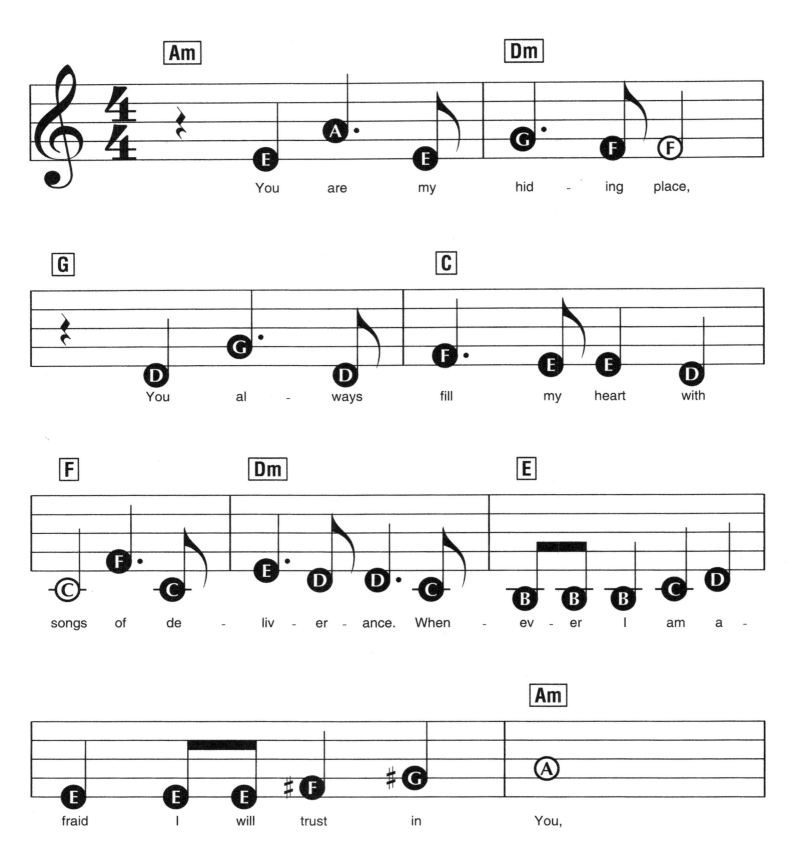

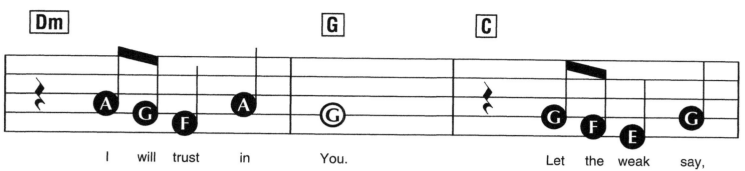

I will trust in You. Let the weak say,

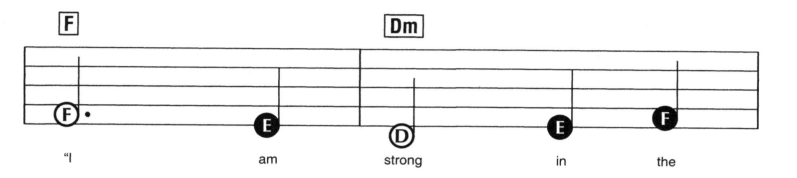

"I am strong in the

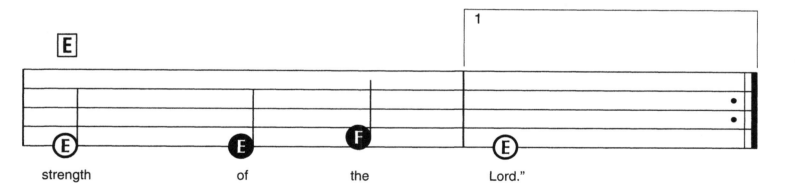

strength of the Lord."

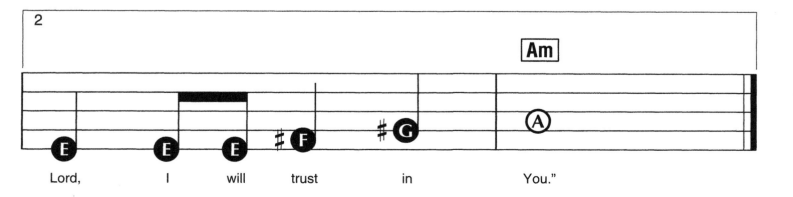

Lord, I will trust in You."

We Bow Down

Registration 8
Rhythm: Waltz

Words and Music by
Twila Paris

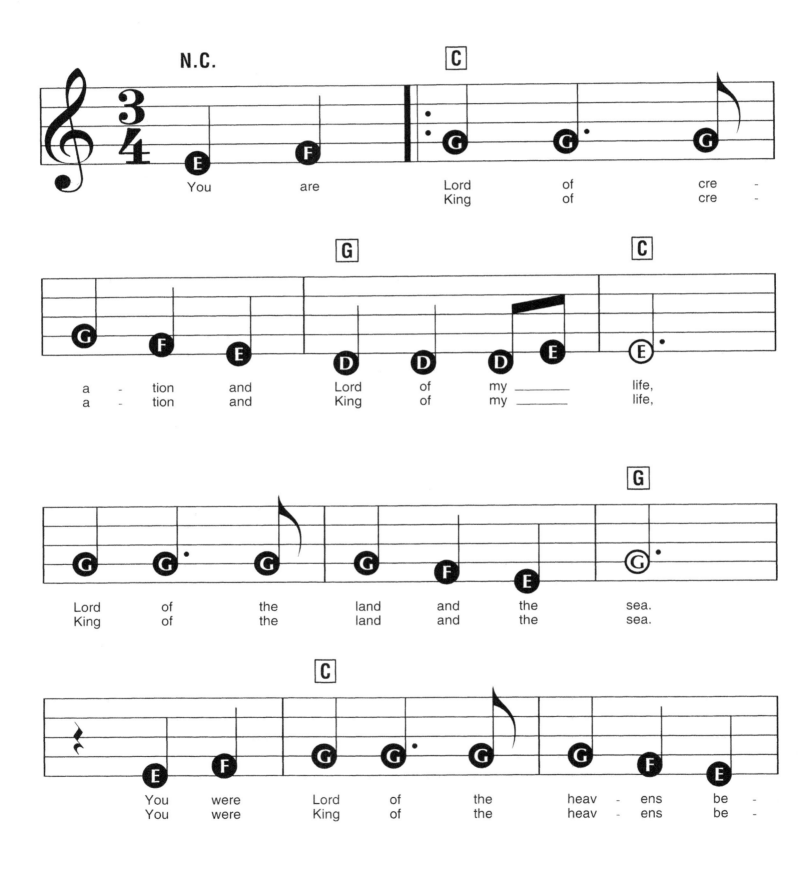

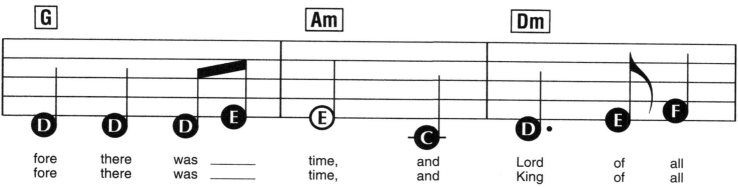

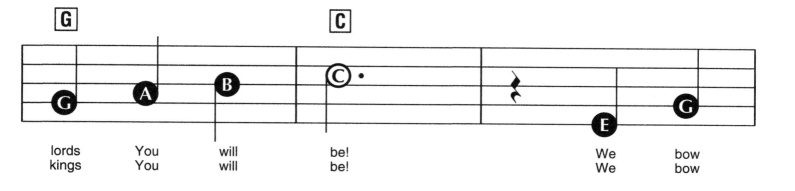

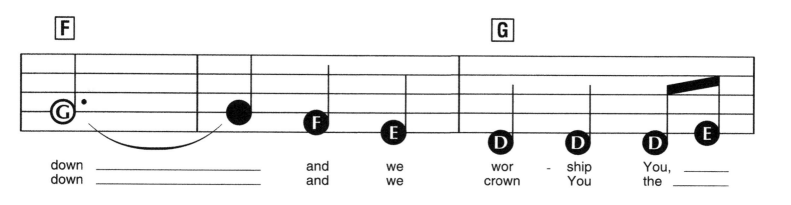

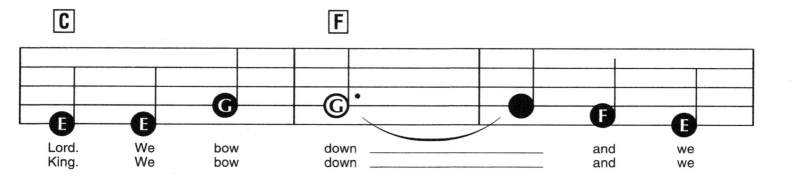

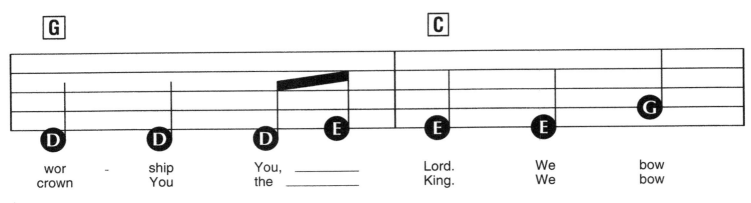

G

wor - ship You, _____ | Lord. We bow
crown You the _____ | King. We bow

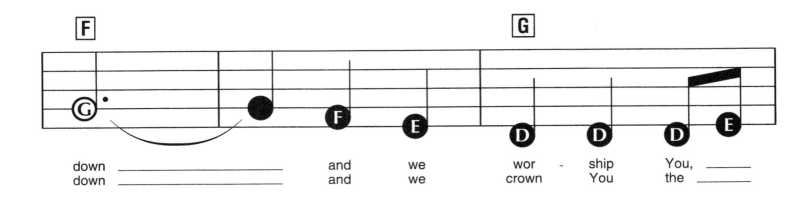

F

down _____ and we | wor - ship You, _____
down _____ and and we | crown You the _____

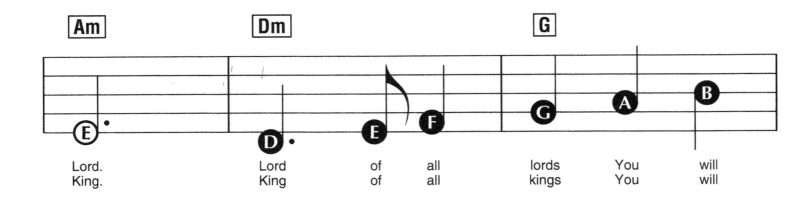

Am Dm G

Lord. | Lord of all | lords You will
King. | King of of all | kings You will

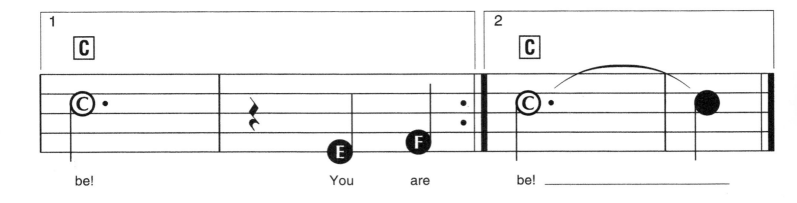

1 C

be! | You are

2 C

be! _____

Registration Guide

- Match the Registration number on the song to the corresponding numbered category below. Select and activate an instrumental sound available on your instrument.

- Choose an automatic rhythm appropriate to the mood and style of the song. (Consult your Owner's Guide for proper operation of automatic rhythm features.)

- Adjust the tempo and volume controls to comfortable settings.

Registration

1	Mellow	Flutes, Clarinet, Oboe, Flugel Horn, Trombone, French Horn, Organ Flutes
2	Ensemble	Brass Section, Sax Section, Wind Ensemble, Full Organ, Theater Organ
3	Strings	Violin, Viola, Cello, Fiddle, String Ensemble, Pizzicato, Organ Strings
4	Guitars	Acoustic/Electric Guitars, Banjo, Mandolin, Dulcimer, Ukulele, Hawaiian Guitar
5	Mallets	Vibraphone, Marimba, Xylophone, Steel Drums, Bells, Celesta, Chimes
6	Liturgical	Pipe Organ, Hand Bells, Vocal Ensemble, Choir, Organ Flutes
7	Bright	Saxophones, Trumpet, Mute Trumpet, Synth Leads, Jazz/Gospel Organs
8	Piano	Piano, Electric Piano, Honky Tonk Piano, Harpsichord, Clavi
9	Novelty	Melodic Percussion, Wah Trumpet, Synth, Whistle, Kazoo, Perc. Organ
10	Bellows	Accordion, French Accordion, Mussette, Harmonica, Pump Organ, Bagpipes